"... as my grandfather said, the river is like poetry. A good poem can be read again to bring back the wonder when it was first read. I thought of my commitment to fly fishing as a kind of poetic exegesis. The more I fished, the more I might be able to uncover the rhythm and structure that makes the river like a poem."

"Perhaps we instinctively know what memories to keep with us. And the memory will find a way to live on."

"... fly fishing is not about being perfect. The key is to let go of what is not important and remember what is. . . . It brings back memories of the thrill of my first trout on the line and time spent with my dad, grandfather, and uncle Joe."

"On the river that day, I felt the affirmation of doing things the right way. My nerves calmed, and my mind relaxed. I became more attuned to traces of movement and sound in the world around me. I sensed a spirit or force that moved through the experience."

"... rivers are national treasures. They pump life into the surrounding environment. They can provoke wonder and stir the imagination. They connect us to the past and lead us into the future."

"... in Montana, fly fishing is not just a sport, it is a way of life."

ARC of the RIVER

A FLY FISHING JOURNEY IN MONTANA

BRENDAN MCCARTHY

RIVERFEET

Riverfeet Press
Livingston, MT/Bemidji, MN/Abingdon, VA
www.riverfeetpress.com

ARC OF THE RIVER
A Fly Fishing Journey in Montana
Brendan McCarthy
Fly Fishing/Family Memoir/Montana
Copyright 2024 © by the author
All rights reserved.
Edited by Daniel J. Rice
ISBN-13: 979-8992007718

This title is available at a special discount to booksellers and libraries. Send inquiries to: riverfeetpress@gmail.com

Cover design by Daniel J. Rice
Cover photos by Brendan McCarthy
Title page photo by Brendan McCarthy
Mayfly illustration by Timothy Goodwin
Typesetting & interior design by Daniel J. Rice

Riverfeet Press is independently owned and operated.

CONTENTS

FOREWORD

Anglers of the fly are an esoteric group of kindred spirits. Our lexicon will baffle the barstool eavesdropper, who may be waiting for key words like *touchdown*, *bitcoin* or *weather* to get involved in a friendly conversation. Believe me, I've turned more heads the opposite direction than those I've converted to discussing the finer points of tippet knot selection or the lifecycle of caddisflies. And we know this. Because each passion in the scope of what we do to occupy our time has the potential to reach the magnitude of obsession. The only requirement is that there's always more to learn. Writing as someone who has been casting flies at fish for over thirty years, in the sport of fly fishing, I can assure you that there is always more to learn. I've yet to max out the receipt of knowledge.

Perhaps this fact, more than the pursuit of a catch, is what brings us back to the river. I cannot write anyone's thoughts other than my own, but what I know to be true about this obsession, is that when I'm reflecting on time spent in the river, it is rarely the fish that receives the majority of my thoughts. It is more often the sound of a riffle, the sight of bedrock at the bottom of a deep pool in crystal clear water, the birds and insects I noticed, or the way a cast felt when the weight of the line released from the rod and rolled forward to land softly and on target.

Every single experienced fly angler I know is a sentimentalist. In fact, being a sentimentalist is the best gauge I know to determine how experienced an angler is at fly fishing. The more sentimental, the more experiences they have had.

McCarthy demonstrates this when he writes: "Fly fishing allows me to forget distractions and instead remember what matters in life." With all of the distractions that can occupy our time, very few of them have the power to center us on what matters in life. It is my opinion that fly fishing should be covered by medical insurance under therapy, because I know of nothing else that equals its cathartic ability to transmute my daily cares and worries into a sense of imperturbability.

As a professional fly fishing guide, a large part of my job is to ensure my clients catch fish. That's what they go into it for, so that is my primary goal. Yet, as someone who values the intimate experiences with a river, the sublime ponderings and soul-cleansing surroundings, I consider it important to pause and point to the osprey on a tree branch, flip some stones and admire the plethora of aquatic life there, or ask them to listen to the silence that occurs while engaged with a cast. Of course, these are all more easily conveyed after they've caught some fish. But I have learned that this is the true value of fly fishing. Therefore, my best days at work occur when, after the day is done, a client says something like, "I didn't even look at my phone once." Or, "That's such a beautiful river, I feel so relaxed."

So when McCarthy first discussed this book with me, I knew he was an angler who had discovered original wisdom in the teachings of many rivers. He's a man who has caught many good fish on a fly, and yet, during our conversations, he never once mentioned a fish he had caught. The attention was focused on his family ties to the sport, the places he remembers, the poetic arc of an angler's life, and the reasons he returned to the river. In his words: "In an upside-down world, I wanted to grab ahold of something meaningful. I sought a place where I could find freedom and tranquility. Fly fishing on a river was that place."

I sensed we had waded upstream on a similar path. While reading his stories about fishing with his dad and grandfather when he was young, and the later stories about going out alone to explore new water, I found myself replaying events from my own life. I believe this is the purpose of good literature—not only does it produce stories of the writer, but, perhaps more importantly, it provides a segue for us to look within ourselves.

It is evident in these stories that fly fishing, for McCarthy, is about more than catching fish, but further, the places it takes us and the memories it creates. Along the way he shares knowledge of technique, from fly selections to reading the water, but these don't receive the lion's share of this text. Instead, his words are focused on the intangible memories that exist like a river in our minds, bending and flowing, teeming with challenges and opportunities, family and fish, and the ever-present quest of seizing our passions. This is a book of wisdom, not only about fly fishing, but inherently more; it touches on the immortal pursuit of becoming better at understanding ourselves.

— Daniel J. Rice, author of *The Unpeopled Season*, and lead guide at Riverfeet Fly Fishing

This book is dedicated to my parents and to Samantha, Billie Grace and Declan.

ARC of the RIVER

A FLY FISHING JOURNEY IN MONTANA

BRENDAN MCCARTHY

"To watch the river flowing, the insects landing and hatching, the places where trout hold, and to insinuate the supple, binding movement of tapered line until, when the combination is right, the line becomes rigid and many of its motions are conceived at the other end."

— Thomas McGuane

INTRODUCTION

During the Covid-19 pandemic, I chose to focus more on fly fishing than I ever had before. A sense of anxiety had taken over the public mood. News channels played stories about the virus. Mask wearing and social distancing became the new normal. In an upside-down world, I wanted to grab ahold of something meaningful. I sought a place where I could find freedom and tranquility. Fly fishing on a river was that place.

As part of my new focus, I decided that I would spend more time fly fishing and also write down old fly fishing stories. I wanted to capture my whole experience of fly fishing from when I first started until the present. I started fly fishing in the early 1990s when I was a young teenager. I lived in New Jersey, but my dad was from Butte, Montana and he grew up fly fishing in Montana. Each summer, he would take me out to fish with my grandfather on the

Big Hole River and other rivers in southwest Montana. I always aspired to be like my dad and grandfather and, for me, fly fishing is about connecting with the past.

By 2020, I was 42 years old and near the age my dad was when he first brought me to Montana. I had also moved from New Jersey to Billings, Montana to work for the U.S. Attorney's Office in 2013 and had fully adapted to life in Montana. But work was busy and I only occasionally had the chance to get out on the river to fish.

The pandemic, though, forced many people to reorder their lives in some way. Like most people, during the early days of the pandemic, in March and April of 2020, my office was shut down and I worked from home. After work I would take long walks with my wife through our neighborhood in Billings and my mind would drift back to fly fishing trips I went on with my dad and grandfather when I was younger. As inspiration for my newfound focus on fly fishing, I also pulled out an old photo from a box tucked away in a bedroom closet. The photo was me as a teenager standing in a swirling river, wearing a black cowboy hat, and holding the first trout I ever caught. Next to me was our guide, Phil Smith – a true cowboy fly fishing guide. The picture also brought back memories of old trips. From there, I would spend time at night or over the weekend and write down those old memories. Writing down those stories provided a short respite from the pandemic and was somewhat cathartic. As I wrote, the focus became not just about fishing, but also where fishing takes place – out on the river.

I also gathered my fly fishing gear and started to plan for some trips when the weather got warmer. I decided that I would carve out time early on the weekends to fish. Living in Billings, the nearby rivers were the Bighorn, Rock Creek, and Stillwater. If I woke up around 5 a.m., I could get to the river early, fish for a few hours and then be home around noon. We also lived near Yellowstone National Park, and I wanted to explore fishing in the Yellowstone High Country.

One thing I learned as I focused more on fly fishing was how overlooked and underappreciated rivers were. They can be hidden and unassuming. We drive past them while heading to the next stop on our busy schedules. But rivers are national treasures. They pump life into the surrounding environment. They can provoke wonder and stir the imagination. They connect us to the past and lead us into the future.

In Montana, majestic rivers extend throughout the state. Each section of Montana has its defining river. Rivers like the Madison, Jefferson and Gallatin stretch throughout the southwest corner. Merriweather Lewis and William Clark named those rivers during their exploration of the West after the country's founding. But the history of those rivers reaches back further than the existence of the United States. Farther west, tucked away in an isolated valley, is the Big Hole River. The Big Hole River is intertwined with the history of my family. The rivers of Montana are all wondrous, but more imagination was poured into creating the Big Hole River.

When I first learned to fly fish, my grandfather told me that the river was like poetry. He moved his hand in a flowing motion imitating water to emphasize his point. I imagined that, for him, a moment on the river brought back memories of his younger days. Days when the river was wild and trout were abundant. And, much like the rhythm of a poem, fly fishing allowed him to understand the patterns and processes of the world. From then on, I learned to listen to the river.

Thirty years have passed since I first began fly fishing in Montana, and I have been lucky to fish many of the rivers throughout the state. Those memories flow like a river. Experience gets swept away as life moves along. Like the river, our paths twist and bend. But along the way, we learn to grow and adapt.

After writing these stories, I realized that fly fishing has taught me how to adapt in life. By looking at fly fishing through a wider lens, I could see how my perspective has shifted over the years. At first, I overcame the fear of a new experience. I then developed a stoic attitude where I learned to accept what I could and could not control. Once I had enough practice, I began to master the art of fly fishing. And mastering a skill that connects you with nature can open the possibility for sublime experience. Finally, fly fishing has become like a ritual that I look forward to each time I go.

My experiences fly fishing the rivers of Montana are different than generations before. So are the challenges we now face. My hope in writing these stories is to capture what it has been like to fly fish in Montana before the experience shifts and we adapt once again.

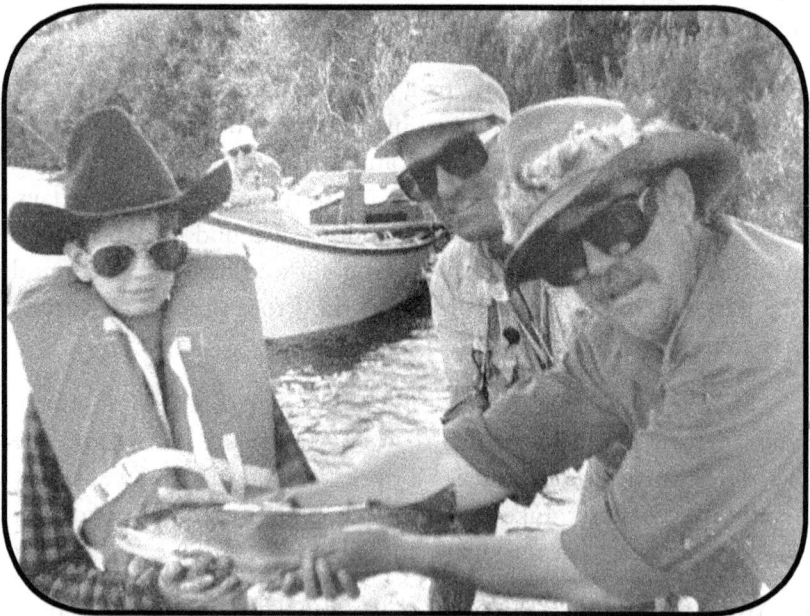

Author on the left with his first fly-caught trout, and legendary guide Phil Smith on the far right.

ONE

THE MEANING OF FLY FISHING

Fly fishing is a deceptively simple sport. It involves the use of a light-weight rod, a colored fly line that is weighted to properly load the rod, and a clear, almost weightless leader to present your fly. Tied to the end of the leader is either a dry fly intended to mimic a floating insect, a nymph intended to imitate an insect larva bobbing over the bottom of the river, or a streamer that is intended to represent a variety of larger prey that fish feed on. To cast a fly rod, you bring the rod back and extend forward smoothly to allow the line to shoot toward your target. Once you get the basic motion down, all you need is practice.

But fly fishing is not like other sports. It does not involve much physical exertion. No score is kept. Two sides do not compete against each other. You hardly even compete against yourself. Instead, your goal is to focus on the line and to be present.

A good fly fisherman is like a good craftsman. Like a craftsman, the only way to improve at fly fishing is to do it repetitively. After a while, you develop a sense of how to cast the line in the same way as a good craftsman develops the sense of how to build the perfect chair or table. The craftsman eventually becomes so adept at the craft that the thought of the tool that he or she uses fades into the background of the mind. For the expert fly fisherman, the act of casting also eventually fades from the conscious mind and he or she only thinks about being fully immersed in the experience.

Fly fishing is now a sport most closely associated with the American West. It was first popularized in Britain where it was known as angling. It became a niche sport in America in the 19th century as depicted in Winslow Homer's tranquil fishing scenes in the Adirondacks. And, the experience of fly fishing was transformed into an artform in the early 20th century by Ernest Hemingway in his semi-autobiographical short stories, the *Big Two-Hearted River*, and in *The Sun Also Rises*. But fly fishing was truly represented by Norman Maclean in his classic Western memoir, *A River Runs Through It*.[1] The book tells the story of Maclean's adventures fly fishing with his brother, Paul, in the 1930s on the Blackfoot River in Montana. Paul's tragic death while the brothers were young men impacted Norman for the rest of his life. The movie, released in 1993, popularized the book and the narrator in the movie recited some of the book's best lines. One of the last lines captures the soul of fly fishing: "Eventually, all things merge into one, and a river runs through it."[1]

The popularity of fly fishing in Montana in the early 20th century corresponded with the closing of the old West. In some respects, the characteristics of the mythic Western figure, the cowboy, were transmuted to the fly fisherman. Like the cowboy, the fly fisherman is resourceful and self-reliant. While the cowboy knew the vast terrain of the plains, the fly fisherman knows the bends and depths of the river. While the cowboy was skillful with his lasso, the fly fisherman is proficient with the cast of the fly line. And, like the cowboy, the fly fisherman is honest, humble and someone who cares for the world.

Fly fishing has now permeated the culture of Montana. Fly shops and outfitters are found in every major city in the state. Small towns like Craig, Melrose and Fort Smith exist solely as fly fishing towns. Ennis calls itself the "Fly Fishing Capital of Montana." Shops throughout the state sell memorabilia emblazoned with images of trout. Restaurants display pictures on walls depicting idyllic fly fishing scenes. Cars and trucks whiz by on the highway with bumper stickers of colorful fish or slogans like "Protect Our Waters."

The law also protects the public access of rivers in Montana. In the 1980s, the state legislature passed a statute to protect the ability to fly fish throughout the state. The Stream Access Law allows an angler to walk anywhere up or down the river if they stay below the highwater mark, so long as they accessed the river legally. The statute also provides that if an angler is floating a river in Montana, they can stop the boat anywhere and get out to fish. The law recognizes that in Montana fly fishing is not just a sport, it is a way of life.

TWO

BUTTE, AMERICA

Before I set foot in the state, I heard many family stories about Montana. For a young kid from New Jersey, it was always interesting to learn about my family's connection to Montana. And any story about my experiences fly fishing in the state would be incomplete without some background about Butte, Montana.

The McCarthy's emigrated to Butte four generations ago. Four generations is enough time for a family to establish a connection to a place. My dad and grandfather were both born and raised in Butte. Before them, my great-grandparents emigrated from Ireland to Butte. Even though I was not raised in Montana, it still feels like home.

Denis McCarthy, or Den as he was called, was my great-grandfather. He was born in Eyeries, Ireland, a small town on the Beara Peninsula in the far southwestern part of County Cork. The Beara Peninsula protrudes from the southernmost tip of Ireland, and on its eastern edge are the blue waters of Bantry Bay. Denis lived on a farm on the north side of the peninsula. As a boy, he would hike from his family's farm to Bantry Bay and set out on a small skiff to fish the deep-blue ocean waters.

In 1912, Denis decided to leave Ireland in search of new opportunity and boarded a ship bound for the United States. Beginning in the late 1890s, thousands of Irish left their homes for the unknown world of Butte, Montana, because they heard that jobs were available in the mines. Those brave immigrants left behind family members whom they would never see again and a country torn apart by famine and war.

Arriving in New York City, businesses displayed "Irish Need Not Apply" signs and people looked down on the Irish as second-class citizens. With what little money he had, Denis boarded a train that took him across a country during enormous industrial growth. He passed through cities in the Midwest and over the Great Plains until he reached the mining capital of the West.

Butte's heyday had been in the early 1900s when the copper mines were in operation and the town was ruled by William Clark, Marcus Daly, and Augustus Heinze – businessmen known as the Copper Kings who controlled all the mining interests. Boisterous Butte was known as the richest hill on earth due to the abundance of raw metals found in the seams under its surface.[2] Those rich mines provided jobs that attracted people from all over the world, including the large wave of immigrants from Ireland. The Copper Kings created grand fortunes from their mining interests. What little wealth remained with the miners seeped through the streets into the pockets of the saloon keepers and brothel hostesses.

Once in Butte, Denis found a place to live in what became known as Ireland's Fifth Provenance with neighborhoods known as Dublin Gulch and Corktown. More Gaelic was spoken in those neighborhoods than anywhere in the world other than Ireland. After finding sparse living quarters, Denis began to work in one of the mines near uptown Butte. But mining was extremely dangerous work. Breathing in the noxious air in the mines gave many miners a deadly lung disease that cut their lives short. Soon Denis realized that it was time to leave the mining business and he eventually landed a position with the Butte Fire Department, which probably saved his life. He worked for the fire department for thirty years. He rose up through the ranks and eventually became the fire chief.

Denis also met Hannah Lowney, another Irish immigrant from West Cork. Hannah and her family immigrated to the United States around the same time as Denis and settled in the same neighborhood near the mines in uptown Butte. They soon planned to get married.

Their wedding was on a beautiful day in June of 1917. But two days later, a cable broke off in the Speculator Mine that set off a terrible fire. The fire swept through the extensive underground tunnels. Miners were trapped in the mineshafts and lost oxygen before they could be rescued. In total, 168 miners lost their lives. It was one of the worst disasters in mining history and it devastated the Butte community.

After the disaster, the miners in Butte went on strike. The United States, however, had entered World War I and needed the mines in Butte to continue to produce copper for the war effort. Martial Law was soon declared. The United States Army, led by future General Omar Bradley, was sent in to overlook the outskirts of the city and to make sure that no further problems occurred. But the rage from the disaster never stopped boiling.

The next year, the citizens of Butte were hit with another catastrophic event – this time a health emergency. In 1919, the Great Influenza swept through the city and killed hundreds of residents including many young children, which had a devastating effect on the mothers in Butte.

All the while, Denis and Hannah shouldered through the hardships and had their first child in 1919. They named their little girl Lois. A year later, Denis and Hannah welcomed another girl, Mable, to the world. In 1923, they had one more child, a boy. They named him George Denis McCarthy and he was my grandfather.

After the end of World War I, servicemen returned to Butte and helped revitalize the city. With mining activity energizing the economy, Butte started to find sounder footing.

The Copper Kings sold their interests in the mines to John D. Rockefeller and the Anaconda Company. The demand for copper and other metal from the mines continued throughout the decade making Butte the richest hill on earth.

The residents of Butte, like most people in the country, fell into severe poverty during the Great Depression. But the United States entrance into World War II, and the military's need for copper, helped Butte's economy bounce back.

From their rough-and-tumble beginnings, the people of Butte formed their own community despite the numerous obstacles they encountered. Homes for families with green yards and room for kids to play were built blocks from the mining headframes. Churches with steeples rising to meet the mountaintops were built on the corners of neighborhood blocks. Children ate cotton candy and rode on rides at Columbia Gardens, an amusement park west of uptown Butte. Restaurants sold a local mix of cuisines influenced by the immigrant cultures. They served pasties, pork chop sandwiches and chop suey. Supper clubs, a staple of the Italian neighborhood, served a dinner steak with a side of homemade spaghetti and raviolis. Butte had its own racetrack, theatres, and a college – the Montana School of Mines. Residents branched out from working in the mines and launched careers in law, medicine, and business. In the early 1900s, Butte was one of the most populated cities west of the Mississippi, second only to San Francisco.

As the midpoint of the 20th century approached, Butte's fortunes dimmed. The Anaconda Company tried to keep up with advances in mining technology and introduced the new process of open pit mining. The company tore down the Columbia Gardens on the outskirts of town and began using equipment to dig into the side of the mountain. It strip-mined deeper and deeper into the mountain creating a large hole. The Anaconda Company could not keep up with cheaper labor and bigger deposits being discovered in places like Arizona and Chile. In the 1970s, they decided to close their doors and walked away from their mines in Butte. Instead of mitigating the damage from pulling out their operations, the company shut off the water pumps that prevented rainwater from accumulating in the mines. Rainwater mixed with metals and eventually formed a toxic manmade lake called the Berkeley Pit. To this day, the Berkeley Pit is one of the largest superfund sites in all of America.

That is a snapshot of the history in Butte before I ever arrived in Montana. It is a study of contrasts. Like many places reliant on natural resources, Butte had a meteoric economic rise followed by a gradual decline.

THREE

INTO THE BIG HOLE VALLEY

I grew up in a small town in New Jersey outside of New York City. The Jersey Shore was not far away. In the summer, families would flock to the shore for a week or two of rest and relaxation. If you did not go to the beach, you could relax at the public pool or one of the pool clubs in town.

When I was in middle school, my parents gave me the freedom to go anywhere I wanted during the summer, as long as my BMX bike could get me there. Most of the time, I would bike to the pool to meet my friends. We would spend the day playing basketball or handball and take breaks for the ice cream truck or to swim.

It never would have occurred to me during those summers in middle school that I could have spent my time fishing on a river in Montana. But, unlike other kids, my dad was from Montana. He had fly fished in Montana as a teenager and he wanted to pass on the experience to me.

In the summer of 1989, I was eleven years old and no longer needed an adult to look after me. I was also apparently old enough to learn how to fly fish. I knew that my dad would sometimes take trips to Montana to fly fish. He would leave for a short weekend with a suitcase and rod case in his hands. That summer I would finally join him and his group on a trip to Montana.

My grandfather, dad and other relatives were all going on the fishing trip. Montana had become a state in 1889, which was one hundred years before the trip. ABC's Wide World of Sports was doing a special program on Montana's Centennial Celebration. To capture the essence of Montana, they decided that they would film a group of fly fisherman during the peak of the fly fishing season. For some reason, they decided to follow my family.

But a few weeks before the trip, I came down with mononucleosis. I laid in bed every day and could not go to school. One thing became clear: I could not get on a flight to Montana. My trip was canceled.

The trip went on without me. They fished the Big Hole River trailed by the camera crew from ABC's Wide World of Sports and caught tons of rainbows and browns.

A few months after the trip, dad received an envelope with a VHS tape in it. He popped the video into the VCR and we gathered around the television in our living room to watch. I saw a fuzzy clip of my dad, grandfather and dad's friend standing near the bank of a river. Someone from behind the camera asked my grandfather how the fishing was. With the brim of his cowboy hat slightly tilted like John Wayne, my grandfather grinned and said that the fishing was only "okay." Even though the fishing had been great, my dad and his friend followed suit and both answered that the fishing had only been okay. After the interviewer left, my dad asked my grandfather why he said that the fishing was just okay. My grandfather smiled and said that if people knew how good the fishing was then they would come out and ruin the experience. To my knowledge, that segment never aired.

Thankfully, fly fishing trips to Montana started to become a yearly occasion in my family, and I finally flew out to Butte the next summer.

Once in Butte, I traced how the city unfurled upwards like one of the cities built on the seven hills of Rome. Driving through Butte, I peered out the window at the flashing neon signs hoisted above restaurants and businesses that lined the streets. At night, the lights of uptown Butte flashed in the distance like Midtown Manhattan.

We stayed at my grandfather's apartment in the Butte Manor, where it seemed like everything was made of concrete. The apartment building looked like a large concrete rectangle. The floors in the hallway were lifeless and hard. A concrete carport jutted out from the building with a parking spot for my grandfather's old Ford pickup truck.

The apartment contained a small living room, three bedrooms in the back and a kitchen to the side. On the coffee table in front of the couch was a stack of playing cards.

After walking into the apartment, we dropped off our bags and sat down in the living room.

My grandfather sat on a couch in the living room and played a hand of solitaire while we caught up. On the television was the Montana nightly news. When the sportscaster came on the screen, I was surprised when he only provided updates on local high school sports instead of professional sports.

After settling in, anticipation filled the air. My dad and grandfather pulled out dark green and musty army duffel bags from the closet. Shiny rods and reels were laid onto the ground. Different sized boots were lined up nearby. Waders hung loosely on the couch in case it got cold on the river the next day. They opened and closed tiny boxes kept in fishing vest pockets. They checked the tiny flies neatly arranged in rows and quietly whispered names and numbers while calculating what they had and what they needed.

My grandfather once ran his own Army surplus business through-out Montana. His store in Butte was along the same hilly street where miners ending their shifts walked home covered in soot. I imagined the old Army equipment that he kept in the apartment reminded him of those days.

Before going to bed, my dad and grandfather had one last thing to take care of – what were they going to do about me? I had never fly fished before. They decided that enough daylight remained for a brief fly casting lesson at a small creek near Anaconda called Racetrack.

Racetrack Creek was not far from the highway. When we got out of the truck, we were surrounded by tall grass and brush. We found a small clearing and started the lesson.

Fly casting has a beautiful simplicity to it. As Norman Maclean's father told him, "It is an art that is performed on a four-count rhythm between ten and two o'clock."[3] For my initial lesson, dad held the rod in one hand and casted into the clearing. I watched the line curl and unfold through the air. It was like watching a cowboy zip a lasso at a steer.

Looking back, that lesson near Racetrack Creek was like a portal to a new world. A world made of more than rod, reel, and line. I was starting to learn the idea of casting. The movement of the rod back-and-forth with the right timing so that the fly lands perfectly at its target. Like a seedling, the idea needs time to grow.

After a few hopeless casts, it became clear that I needed more practice. I needed to be on the river to watch the fly, mend the line and set the hook. We packed up the rods and gear and drove in the dark back to Butte.

In the morning, my alarm buzzed and I stared blankly at the flashing red numbers. I was not prepared for the shock of 5:30 am. Dad said I only had five minutes to shower and then we were leaving. I got out of the shower and put on a long-sleeved shirt and jeans because I knew that it was going to be cold out.

It was silent and pitch black as we carried our fishing equipment to the truck. For June, it was also unseasonably cold. We drove up Harrison Avenue and took the exit to get onto I-90. To my right, I saw a shining orb atop the dark silhouette of the ragged-edges of the mountain range that surrounds Butte. In the dark, it is difficult to see that the statue is Our Lady of the Rockies – a replica of the Virgin Mary built on a dare after the mines shut down and economy collapsed.

Our Lady of the Rockies stands almost ninety feet tall and weighs around eighty tons. It was built in the late 1970s by a Butte welder named Bob O'Bill with the assistance of volunteers. O'Bill had the vision to build the statue after his wife was diagnosed with cancer. In his prayers, he told Mary that he would build a statute in her honor if his wife survived. When his wife survived, O'Bill repaid his debt. He and his volunteers crafted enormous metal segments for the statue and planned to assemble them once they were transported to the top of the mountain. His plan was complicated by the fact that no roads ran to the top of the mountain.

Knowing they had connections in Washington, D.C., the community leaders reached out to my grandfather for help. My grandfather contacted his friend and mentor, Senator Mike Mansfield, who had been the longest serving Senate Majority leader. Mansfield also once worked in the copper mines in Butte, slugging ore after service in World War I. Mansfield told my grandfather to call Senators John Stennis and John Melcher and tell them that it would be considered a personal favor for Mansfield if the senators could help the City of Butte get the statue to the top of the Continental Divide. The senators then arranged for the Army Corp of Engineers to provide a Sikorsky Skycrane helicopter that was used to transport the metal segments from a Butte work yard to the top of the mountain. Day-by-day metal segments dangled from the bottom of the helicopter as they were airlifted up the mountain, and construction was eventually completed.

A few years later, groups began to challenge the use of the Army to help build the statue on First Amendment grounds. Caving into pressure, the Army sent Butte an invoice back-charging it hundreds of thousands of dollars for its service. Butte, however, did not have enough money to cover the bill. So the city again turned to my grandfather for advice. My grandfather drafted a letter to the Army acknowledging a mistake in using the Army's services to help construct the statue. But he cleverly recommended that the Army remedy the issue by transporting the metal segments back down the mountain. The Army relented and never sent Butte another bill.

As we continued our drive to the river, we entered the Big Hole Valley. The Big Hole Valley is picturesque and isolated. Thousands of years ago, receding glaciers cut through the landscape and carved out the valley. In the valley, cattle grazed on hay in wide open spaces, and snow-capped mountains rose in the distance. When I first drove through it, I would force my eyelids open as wide as possible. The sky was so big and I wanted to capture it all. The valley also has a significant number of large mosquitoes in the summer, which helps to keep the tourist population at bay.

Native American tribes inhabited the Big Hole Valley for thousands of years. European settlers started to slowly migrate into the valley in the 1700s. Lewis and Clark reached the mouth of the Big Hole River in August 1805. After Lewis and Clark's expedition, more settlers, trappers, and traders began moving into the western territory of the country. The constant encroachment eventually led to conflicts with the tribes.

In 1877, the U.S. Army attacked the Nez Perce, a tribe from Idaho, west of where the town of Wisdom, Montana is now located near the river. The Nez Perce had tried to leave their native lands near Idaho in hopes of finding a safer place to live in Canada. Their leader, Chief Joseph, took them on a path that led through Montana. They decided to avoid a direct route to Canada through the Bitterroot Valley out of fear of clashing with the Missoula Militia. Their plan was to loop further south and, thereafter, head north through the eastern plains of Montana.[4]

In the summer of 1877, the Nez Perce set up teepees along the banks of the upper Big Hole River where the river widens. The warriors went out to hunt. The old sought treatment for their ailments and mothers tended to their young children.

One morning, the U.S. Army suddenly ambushed the Nez Perce's encampment. They set fire to the teepees and killed anyone in their sight. The warriors did not have time to gather their weapons and only engaged the soldiers with fists or rocks they could throw before retreating.

Soon, though, the warriors returned to save the women and children. They fended off the soldiers and pushed them back into the woods. From there, the battle became a standoff. With no water or food, the Army had to retreat.

The Nez Perce suffered several casualties during the ambush. But they eventually regrouped. Chief Joseph led them through what is now Yellowstone National Park and back up into Montana and the land of the Crow Indians. The Nez Perce traveled only a few miles from the Canadian Border near Bear's Paw until they were captured by the Army and forced onto a reservation.

In the early morning light, we passed the exit to Highway 43, which snaked westward next to the Big Hole River and led to the town of Wisdom and the Big Hole Battlefield. We continued south, past Maiden Rock Road – one of the roads that leads to the river.

After Maiden Rock Road, we took the exit for Melrose and drove the one-lane highway through town. To the left were homes, an old hotel, and train tracks leading off into the distance. To the right was a restaurant and fly shop and farther down another restaurant and fly shop. We parked in front of the last fly shop in Melrose. Stepping out of the car, the only sound we heard were the cattle chewing and bellowing on the nearby ranches.

Arriving at the fly shop at 6:30 am meant that we could get on the river right when the sun was rising. The fishing was typically better during those early morning hours.

The fly shop in Melrose was the perfect fly shop. It looked like a hideout for Butch Cassidy's Hole in the Wall gang. It was a cabin with brown logs stacked upon each other and a covered wooden porch held up by more giant brown logs. The wooden planks on the steps to the porch creaked when we stepped on them.

Inside the shop, we met with the owner and our guides, one of whom was Phil Smith. I do not know how long Phil had been guiding on the Big Hole at that time, but he was an acclaimed guide and his knowledge of the river was second-to-none. When he spotted me, Phil reached out his big hand, smiled and said "Howdy." He said he had fished with my dad and grandfather for years and he would help get me all set up. He showed me some of the flies and explained how some float on the top and some sink below the water. I peeked into the boxes holding all the different patterns of flies. The flies were a mix of brown, white, red, yellow, and purple colors and some were tiny and some had big, fluffy wings.

While we filled out our fishing licenses, my dad and my grandfather chatted with the guides about the different flies that had been working. The guides told stories about some of the bigger fish they had caught earlier in the season and the current conditions of the river. It looked like it would be a good day of fishing for us.

To get to the river, we hopped into Phil's old pickup truck. The white drift boat we would fish in was hitched to the back. We drove on the paved road through town and bumped along a local dirt road until we arrived at the fishing access site.

The water on the Big Hole flows freely with no dam controlling its level. The snow that melts in the mountains above Jackson during the warm days of early spring trickles down the mountain. The mountain streams connect with the river, and the river rises and widens during the spring. The water moves east and flows into the Jefferson River, then meets the Missouri River, where it later rolls into the Mississippi River and eventually empties into the ocean.

The Big Hole River is also known for its variety of different insect hatches. At different times, stonefly, mayfly, and caddis hatches appear. But the most anticipated hatch, the one the big trout go crazy for, is the salmonfly hatch. Salmonfiles are super-sized, giant-winged flies that monster trout gobble down sometime in the later weeks of June each year.

Signs led to access sites at Maiden Rock, Divide, Salmon Fly, Brown's Bridge and Glen along the river. After fishing the river for decades, each site evokes its own memory. We fished the lower section of the river that day, somewhere from Melrose to Divide.

At the access site, everyone got their rods rigged up. Reels were tightened on the rods, lines were looped through holes on the rods, and rods were handed over to the guides to put the flies on. I sprayed mosquito repellent all over my skin and clothes.

Phil backed the pickup truck down the boat ramp and pulled the boat close so we could get in. Dad brought a regular orange safety vest that I had to put on. It looked like the kind you would find on a dingy. After I put it on, it hung in front of me like a prop. Before getting in, I was reminded that if I fell in the water, I had to keep my legs in front of me and head up so that I could see any rocks. If I did not, my head could hit a rock and I would drown.

They put me in the front of the boat so they could see what I was doing, and my dad was in the back of the boat. Phil was in the middle rowing and instructing us where to cast. It was my first time out of the river and I felt nervous. I kept trying, but mostly my line would get tangled like it did on Racetrack Creek. Phil patiently spent most of the day untangling my line and putting on new flies, but I hardly progressed. Sometimes I paused and watched everyone else fish.

Around noon, we pulled the drift boats over and sat on the rocky bank and ate sandwiches for lunch.

During part of the trip, I switched boats and got the chance to fish with my grandfather. My grandfather was in his sixties, but he remained vigorous. He played football and boxed when he was younger, and his large hands dropped by his sides like sledgehammers.

He had studied engineering in college, and the Army sent him to Virginia Polytechnic in Blacksburg to continue work on his engineering degree during World War II. Had the war not ended, he would have worked on the Manhattan Project. After the war, he started McCarthy Engineering in Butte and, among other projects, surveyed several large ranches in the Big Hole Valley. The ranchers would let him access the Big Hole River, and he would leave a few of the trout at the rancher's doorstep in return. That was the way things used to be.

He also got involved in politics and won an election as the county surveyor for Silver Bow County, a powerful position in Butte. He then won a second term with a campaign slogan of Veteran-Experienced-Capable. His political acumen led to him running campaigns for other candidates. In 1959, he met a young senator from Massachusetts, John F. Kennedy, who impressed him. My grandfather helped manage Kennedy's campaign in Montana and other Western states. When Kennedy won, my grandfather moved his family of five kids to Washington, D.C. to work at the Department of Defense. During the Johnson Administration, my grandfather managed congressional relations for the Office of Economic Opportunity, and he helped guide the most impactful anti-poverty legislation ever passed through Congress.

On the river, my grandfather smiled and gently cast the line into the water. Phil rowed us in-and-out of good spots. Every so often, a flourish of activity would occur and my grandfather would have another fish on the line.

Phil provided a few helpful tips on how to cast, but I did not have the ability to put them into action. Instead, the best I could do was watch and learn from my grandfather.

At one point, Phil pulled the drift boat over to the bank after my grandfather caught a nice-sized rainbow trout. It was one my grandfather wanted to keep. He had me get out of the boat and brought me to his side to show me what it was like to clean out a trout. He banged the fish's head against a rock to knock it out and pulled out a serrated knife. He cut a deep incision in the center of the trout's belly. When he opened the fish up like a wallet, I saw the pink insides of the trout and rows of thin bones. The trout's guts were wiped away and it was placed on ice in the creel.

I knew that fish were meant for eating and the whole process was natural. Even so, fear and awe radiated through me as I took in the whole experience. I had never been on a river before much less seen a fish banged against a rock and cut open. The feeling of trepidation was my first reaction to fly fishing and it stayed with me until I gained some mastery over how to fish.

After getting off the river, we changed out of our wet clothes and headed back to Butte for dinner at the Copper King Mansion. The Copper King Mansion was built by William A. Clark – one of the original Copper Kings and richest men in the country during his lifetime. While we ate dinner in the mansion, Clark's daughter, Huguette, lived alone in New York City. She lived in an apartment on Fifth Avenue surrounded by a large collection of artwork and dolls worth millions of dollars. If only the miners knew that their blood, sweat, and misery went to fund that collection.

At dinner, we ate, drank, and told stories. My grandfather sat at the head of a long dining table under the ornate chandelier. Everyone's attention turned to him as he began to tell the first story of the night.

His story focused on his uncle, Con Lowney. Con was the older brother of my grandfather's mother, Hannah. He had emigrated from Ireland to Butte before other members of the Lowney family. Con had never married and he became like a second father to my grandfather.

In Butte, Con started out working in the mines. But, like my great-grandfather Denis, he quickly learned that mining was a dangerous profession. He escaped mining and became a barber, setting up his barber shop in the basement of The Miners Union Building in uptown Butte. Because many of his customers were members of the miner's union, Con became active in the union and witnessed the poor treatment of Butte's miners and their families. In 1914, the mining companies blew up both The Miners Union Building and Con's barber shop, either as a warning, or in retaliation for their activity.

After the Speculator Mine disaster, the miners went on strike and Con was one of the leading union activists. For his work, Con and four to five other union activists were targeted for execution by the mine owners. While the Butte miners were on strike, a national workers organization called the International Workers of the World (or "Wobblies" as they were known), decided to send one of their spokespeople, Frank Little, to Butte to give a major speech. Con warned Little that it was not the right time to be in Butte and he was on a list of people to be executed. Little remained in Butte anyway and Con never understood why.

During the first night Little stayed in Butte, two cars full of men with guns pulled up outside of Little's hotel. They broke into Little's room, dragged him from the building and tied him to the back of the car. They drove him through town behind the car as his body scraped the pavement. They took him out to the nearby train trestle bridge below uptown Butte and hung him. They affixed the sign 3-7-77 on his body. To this day, the killers of Frank Little have never been identified and certainly were never brought to justice.

The same evening Little was hung, the killers stormed into the apartment building in uptown Butte where Con lived. Knowing his life was in danger, Con boarded himself up in his apartment. He sat in a wooden chair in the middle of the living room and gripped a revolver in each hand. When he looked through the window in his dark room, he recognized the men who exited their cars and approached his building. He steadied his nerves and cocked the trigger on each revolver. He listened for the sound of boots as the killers walked up the stairwell and neared his door. When they were within earshot, Con shouted that every man would meet his maker from one of his bullets if they tried to enter the room. After his deadly warning, the hallway went silent, and Con heard bootsteps fading down the hall.

When my grandfather told a Con story, he would adopt an Irish accent to imitate the distinct sound of Con's voice. In the story that he told that night, my grandfather was running his Army surplus store and Con worked in the store a few days a week.

One morning, a customer came into the store looking for new shoes. For over an hour, the customer asked for this pair of shoes and that pair of shoes, but he found something wrong with each shoe he tried.

By the time the customer had asked to try on his twentieth or so pair, Con was at his wit's end, but he desperately wanted to make the sale. When the customer tried on the last pair, Con showered him with praise.

"Oh, what a fine-looking shoe! Fits you perfectly! Will you be buying those, now?" Con asked in his Irish brogue.

When the customer once again shook his head and rejected a sale, Con lost his temper. He picked up the shoes and threw them at the customer's head as he chased him out of the store. As the door swung open, Con added insult to injury and hurled some curse words at the customer.

Unfortunately for the customer, he had forgotten a pair of glasses in the shop. Time passed by, but the customer had not returned. Hours later, Con peeked out the front window and saw the customer sheepishly standing across the street. Con graciously waved him back in.

He brought the customer to the front of the store where the glasses were sitting on the counter. The glasses were placed next to two boxes of shoes. While handing the customer his glasses back, Con pushed forward a box of shoes that the customer had tried on.

"And you'll be buying these, now, won't ya?" Con said.

The customer, his glasses within reach, nodded his head in affirmation.

Con next picked up another pair of shoes and put those on top of the first pair.

"And you'll be buying these shoes too, won't ya?"

The customer again nodded his head up-and-down. Finally, without a word, Con placed the glasses on top of the shoe boxes.

"I believe you'll be needing these too," he said.

The customer paid for both pairs of shoes and walked out of the store without looking back.

At the dinner table, everyone laughed and drank from their glasses. We cut up more pieces of our dinner steaks and waited for the next story.

As the night wound down, my grandfather told one other story about Con. Before he died, Con was sick and visited a priest at a church in Butte. The priest knew Con from town, but he also knew that Con never went to church. Con confessed to the priest that he had strayed from the church during his life and had not attended mass in years. The priest nodded his head. But he wanted to come back to God before he died and asked the priest for last rites. The priest noted that it would be unusual to grant such a request, and he asked Con why he was returning to the church after so long an absence. A moment passed as Con calculated a response. Then Con admitted that he was not much of a believer in the Almighty. But, given the circumstances, he said: "I don't want to be taking any chances."

At dinner, I learned that fly fishing in Montana was about more than just the fishing. It was about keeping the past alive. My grand-father was telling stories about events that happened more than a half-a-century ago. And he told them like they had just happened. Surrounded by him were his sons and grandson and lifelong friends. Now I knew why fly fishing was so important to my dad.

Before the night ended, one of our family friends went into his truck and brought back a black ten-gallon cowboy hat. He said he never wore it and I could have it. I did not know what I would do with a cowboy hat back home in New Jersey and it did not quite fit. But if I accepted, I would be part of the group. So I did.

Our group could have stayed up all night telling stores, but we were all tired from a day on the river, plus we had to get up again before dawn for another day of fishing. With our stomachs full, we drove back to the Butte Manor for some rest.

FOUR

FISHING THE MADISON

The next morning, I woke up again before dawn for another day of fly fishing. I showered and quickly got dressed. In no time, we were on the road in the dark while Butte slept.

We were heading southeast to fish the Madison River near Ennis that day. The Madison River forms at the confluence of the Firehole and Gibbon Rivers in Yellowstone National Park. It flows northwest into Montana through Hebgen Lake and into the Madison Valley. The river ends near Three Forks, Montana where it joins with the Gallatin and Jefferson Rivers to form the Missouri River.

The best view of the Madison Valley is driving down from Virginia City. Virginia City is an old mining town nestled in the mountains on the western edge of the valley. Miners flocked to Virginia City in 1863 when gold was first discovered nearby by prospectors. Virginia City experienced an economic boom and a frontier town soon developed. But no law authority existed in the town during those early days. Criminals, known as road agents, robbed and murdered many prospectors along the trails into town. To establish order, the townsmen formed their own vigilante group. And they captured and hung several of the road agents. The townsmen also affixed the warning sign "3-7-77" to the dead road agents' bodies. The same sign that was later affixed on Frank Little. The actual origins of the "3-7-77" sign are mysteriously unknown, but it is said to be the exact dimensions of a coffin.

When the Montana Territory was formed in 1864, President Abraham Lincoln appointed his friend and Irishman, Thomas Francis Meagher, as the territory's first governor. Meagher was born in Waterford, Ireland and had been banished from Ireland because of his involvement in an independence movement known as the Young Irelanders. Instead of executing him for treason, Great Britain sent Meagher to a penal colony in Australia called Van Diemen's Land.

After a daring escape from Van Diemen's Land, Meagher traveled by ship across the world to New York City. Soon after Meagher emigrated to the United States, the country was torn apart by shots fired at Fort Sumter in South Carolina and the beginning of the Civil War. The first soldier killed was an unlucky Irishman from Skibbereen.

A soldier at heart, Meagher volunteered for the Union Army and rose through the ranks to become Brigadier General of the Irish Brigade. Meagher convinced thousands of Irish emigres to join his unit and the Irish Brigade became one of the most successful and fiercest units in the Union Army. They were noted for bravery in the battlefields of Antietam and Fredericksburg. Given his units significance in the war effort, Meagher soon became a confidante of Abraham Lincoln. Lincoln knew that the North would not have prevailed absent the courage of the Irish Brigade.

Due to Meagher's accomplishments, Lincoln promoted him to

one last assignment – the provisional governor of the Montana Territory. Meagher journeyed across the country to Virginia City, the capital of the Montana territory, to assume command as governor. Even though the frigid climate high in the mountains was much different than Ireland's weather, Meagher's goal was to one day see Montana become a New Ireland – a place where the people of Irish descent could live free.

Meagher was never able to accomplish his dreams while he was alive. The vigilantes who had run the road agents out of town did not appreciate a young Irishmen taking over as the territory's governor. Within a few years, Meagher died in a suspicious accident after allegedly falling off a steamboat on the Missouri River near Fort Benton, Montana. No one ever determined the cause of death. But it probably was not an inadvertent fall. Most likely one of the vigilantes or someone directed by them pushed Meagher toward his death.[5]

While Meagher was never able to accomplish his dream of establishing a New Ireland in Montana during his lifetime, the dream never died. By the beginning of the 20th century, Irish immigrants who made Butte their home had successfully turned it into the closest version of a New Ireland in the world.

. . .

On the Madison River that day, we fished with Phil Smith as our guide and I spent most of the day fishing with my dad and his good friend, Jim. I again had trouble casting. I took the line too far back and did not accelerate far enough forward. I could not get the rhythm down. Instead of catching anything, I spent much of the day soaking in the environment and trying to learn from everyone else who fished.

After a midday break for lunch on the bank of the river, I switched to the front of the boat where Phil could see me cast. Phil had on an old cowboy hat with the felt strip circled around it that contained an array of different flies. In between casts, Phil would drop the drift boat's anchor and change out flies from the collection on the felt strip. Once rigged up, Phil would dig the oars deep into the water and move us closer to good pools of water.

At one bend in the river, Phil pulled the boat over. He knew that fish would be biting if we casted out into the current. Phil helped me get out of the boat while dad waded into the river and started casting into the riffles. Suddenly dad jolted back. His rod tip bent down and he moved it side-to-side while walking back to the bank.

Without much warning, dad placed a fly rod with a fish on the line in my hands. Phil stood behind my back shoulder and provided instructions. I kept the line tight while the fish kept fighting on the other end. It took all my strength to keep the rod upright.

At one point, Phil grabbed ahold of the rod to keep the line tight and reeled it in slowly. The fish was only a few feet away from me and I could see its head and tail flipping as it darted back-and-forth. With the line almost fully in, Phil helped me lift the rod higher and he swooped underneath it with a net. Like a baby in a swaddle, a silver rainbow trout with a stroke of red across its side rested at the bottom of the net.

As Phil picked the rainbow out of the net, dad pulled out a yellow disposable camera. Phil held the fish in his hands, I placed my hands underneath it, and we all squeezed together as dad snapped the picture.

We had the pictures developed when we returned home to New Jersey. My mom framed the one of me with the rainbow trout standing next to Phil. In the picture, I had on the black cowboy hat our friend had gifted me the night before. I have brought that picture with me wherever I moved. Whenever I look at it, I am transported back to the experience of maneuvering the line back-and-forth with Phil's help to bring in that first rainbow trout.

Months after that trip, seasons changed, daylight slowly faded and Melrose became deserted in winter. It must have been difficult for the few people that worked in town like Phil Smith. I remember one winter night reclining on a couch in the living room at our home in New Jersey. My dad sat on a chair in the kitchen with a cordless phone pressed to his ear. My grandfather was speaking to him on the other end of the line. They talked in hushed tones about a piece of bad news.

After the call, I learned that Phil Smith had killed himself. My dad kept most of the details to himself. I tried to speculate about what happened. Maybe Phil received a terrible health diagnosis or perhaps a long relationship had ended. He had seemed happy on the river only a few months ago. He had patiently given me tips on how to fish and he smiled when I pulled in my first fish. But now he was gone.

FIVE

UP IN THE PINTLER MOUNTAINS

The next summer, dad planned a trip to fish the upper lakes in the Pintler Mountains near Butte. To get to the upper lakes, we would first meet at the outfitter's lodge and ride by horseback up to the campsite. We would be joined on the trip by my grandfather and my uncle, as well as my dad's friend, Jim, and his two daughters.

After flying into Butte, we drove into the mountains the next day. We took a winding, dirt road through the forest to a deserted lodge. Staying in a fishing lodge in Montana is as close as you will come to staying in a castle in medieval times. Fishing lodges in the mountains are isolated, remote, and overly spacious places. When you have a fishing lodge almost to yourself, you feel like the king of the castle.

At the lodge, my grandfather felt lightheaded. A few years before, he had been diagnosed with an irregular heartbeat. If anything happened to him on the way to or up at the campsite, they could not have brought him to a hospital in time. My uncle, a doctor, suggested that he not go up. My grandfather relented and decided to stay back at the lodge with my uncle and wait for us to return.

With two of our party members dropping out, the rest of us rose early in the morning and met our guides – a couple young cowboys who knew horses and those mountains well. I had never ridden a horse before, but I concentrated as much as I could on our instructions. I digested how to place my foot in the stirrup, what to do if the horse bucked, and how to go faster.

I got on my horse and we trotted forward into the wilderness with the ropes in my hand. One cowboy took the lead and the other stayed in the back of the pack.

On the way up, the sun shined and the horses steadily strutted up the winding path. Some parts of the path were as narrow as the cliff in Charlie Russell's *Scouting the Enemy*. I could hear the horse's hooves clip-clob on the rocks along the path.

At the campsite, white tents were lined up in a row. In front of the tents was a deep pit for a fire. The horses rested nearby. The cowboys orderly unpacked our supplies. The depths of the forest surrounded the campsite.

After unpacking, we grabbed our rods and walked along a narrow dirt trail to a secluded lake. Thousands of years before, large glaciers had sliced through the mountains and created almost unpassable boulders that surrounded both sides of the lake. The water in the lake and the sky seemed to connect as one.

Lake fly fishing was different than stream fishing. The water was deep and placid in a mountain lake. Trout that had never wandered down the stream rested near the lake bed. Some trout grew into giants in the upper lakes.

We spent a couple hours fishing. Everyone staked out a spot along the shore. Everyone else also caught some fish, but I was skunked again. It was nothing to be too upset about because we had more fishing to do in the morning.

We returned to camp and the scent of food being grilled on cast iron skillets over the fire. After changing out of our cold clothes, we joined everyone else to warm ourselves by the fire and grab a plate for dinner.

One of our cowboy guides was a young cowboy named Rooster. He wore a worn-out cowboy hat and a shiny belt buckle. He packed some chewing tobacco under his lip. He smiled and seemed happy to be in the mountains.

As we sat around the campfire, Rooster talked about life as a young rodeo cowboy. His father, Benny Reynolds, was a legendary rodeo star in Montana. Benny Reynolds won more than 360 championship buckles during his career and he qualified eleven times for the National Finals Rodeo.[6] In 1961, he won the World All Around Champion Cowboy title and he was inducted into the Pro Rodeo Hall of Fame in 1993.[7] To be in the rodeo, you must be impervious to pain. Benny Reynolds grew up on a ranch. Rooster said that, when his dad was a kid, his brothers would put his head in a vice and turn the screws until he relented. But Benny was more than tough. Montana Poet Laureate, Mark Gibbons, met Benny Reynolds once in the Big Hole Valley. He wrote that Benny was everything a young boy would want his hero to be, "… gentle, kind, all modesty, humility, and strength."[8]

Rooster grew up on the family ranch near Twin Bridges and learned how to be a cowboy from his father. But when he told his stories, you could sense how times had slowly changed.

After dinner, we packed up all our dirty plates in a bag and one of the guides tied it up with a rope and slung it over a tree away from our campsite so that bears would not come near. We splashed the fire with whatever beverage we had left to put it out. As the embers sizzled, we walked back to each of our tents. On the way back to the tent, I looked up at the sprawling galaxy of stars scattered throughout the dark sky.

I was too scared of a grizzly bear pacing outside our tent or a pack of wolves circling around us to get much sleep. Plus, a sleeping bag over a cot is a lot less comfortable than the mattress and box springs that I had become accustomed to. So I tossed and turned throughout the night until I heard the patter of raindrops falling on our tent in the early morning hours.

Once the rain started to fall harder, I knew that our plans of an early breakfast and fishing at sunrise had been cancelled. Instead, dad and Jim huddled with the guides and decided to pack up early and head back down the mountain.

I fortunately did have a rain jacket to put on, but I was not much help packing up the heavy camping gear that we had. The only thing I had to do was to get on the horse and make sure it got me back down the mountain to our lodge.

We must have angered the mountain gods because even the relatively easy goal of making it down the mountain became immensely more difficult. From a drip to a steady pour, the rain started to pummel down from the sky. Thunder boomed and lighting cracked in the distance. One horse sprinted right off when a cowboy tried to corral it. Another horse jolted so high in the air that it looked like Frederic Remington's *Broncho Buster* in action.

Trying to proceed forward in a rain and hailstorm driving against us made little sense, but we did not have much of an alternative. Without a fire, we could not make our eggs and bacon or heat up coffee for the adults. We could either face the storm that would not relent, or we could wait to face it later when we would be hungrier and wetter.

We chose the first option and proceeded step-by-step back to the trail that had got us up to the camp. I had to kick my horse on the side in the ribs to get him to keep moving. The horse whinnied and thrust his head side-to-side during the descent, and I steadied him with the rope.

The narrow trail along the steep edge had been tricky to pass the day before. Now it was slippery and more dangerous. The rain drenched and seeped through my coat, jeans, and socks. Rain soon turned to hail and I kept my head down so that the icy pebbles would bounce off the top of my head instead of my face. I felt the cold and the wet deep in my bones. My muscles turned turgid and useless and I gripped the rope with the bones of my fingers.

The trip down the mountain felt twice as long as the trip up. But we pushed forward through the elements like the cowpunchers stuck in the blizzard trying to make it back to the cabin in Wallace Stegner's *Genesis*.[9] It took us almost the whole day to make it back. Finally, we did.

Back at the lodge, my grandfather and uncle chuckled as they saw us straggle into view. We thawed our bones near the fire, and a warm shower before dinner never felt better.

Although the elements treated us poorly, I nonetheless enjoyed our trip. The bitter cold horseback ride down the mountain only reminded me of how lucky I was to get a sunny day of fishing at the lake the day before. Prior leaving, we thanked our cowboy guides and headed back to Butte.

After that trip, I started to develop my own philosophy about fly fishing and life, which was basically a stoic one. I started to learn that we have the power to control how we respond to things that happen to us. In other words, nothing happens to us that we cannot handle. In a split second after each experience, we choose how we will react.

As a result, we should focus on the things we can control, and not worry about the things that we can *not*. If something bad happens or someone insults us, we should not get upset about it. Instead, we should take a moment and not let it affect us. And, in the case of someone who insults us, those insults reflect that person's bad character more than they say anything about us.

Traveling down the mountain in a hailstorm, I found that there was no point in getting frustrated. And in pushing away that frustration, I took the first steps in gaining control over negative emotions.

I also learned that emotions can sometimes cloud our thought and by pushing away negative emotions, I felt more connected to the natural world around me. And, in feeling more connected to nature, I could pick up the natural patterns and processes that run through the world.

When I returned to New Jersey, I sometimes escaped back to my time in Montana by watching Western movies with stoic heroes. In the 1990s, the era of the cowboy Western had long since closed. I was too young to watch John Wayne or Gary Cooper movies. But I had watched some more modern Westerns like *The Outlaw Josey Wales* and *Butch Cassidy and the Sundance Kid*. I also loved the movie *Young Guns* about Billy the Kid and his gang.

Young Guns was followed by other great movies set in the West – *Tombstone*, *Legends of the Fall*, and *Unforgiven*. But it was in a movie appreciation class in high school that I watched the Western movie that I liked the best – *Pale Rider* with Clint Eastwood. The title of the movie derived from the four riders of the Apocalypse passage from the Book of Revelation: "And I looked, and behold a pale horse: and his name that sat on him was Death, and Hell followed with him." In the movie, Eastwood played a preacher who rode into a small gold mining community in California and appeared to be escaping something in his past or perhaps was only an apparition himself. He befriended a mother and daughter in the mining community. The mining baron in the nearby town sent his men to destroy the mining community and terrorize the miners. Like any good Western movie, the circumstances called for a stoic hero to face down the bad guys. The Preacher was that hero. He rode into town on a pale horse. Like the biblical passage, he represented Death. He and his friend, Hull, exacted revenge on the mining baron and his henchmen. And order was restored in the community.

After watching *Pale Rider*, I wanted be like the Preacher. I mimicked Eastwood's dark glare. And I copied his purposeful walk. I wanted to be the stoic hero.

I had a chance to practice my Eastwood impersonation on a few summer fly fishing trips to Montana during high school. I still had that ten-gallon black Stetson hat that I got on our first fly fishing trip. As I got older, the hat fit better. I could wear the hat with the brim pulled close over my forehead to make me seem more formidable. After a day on the river, I would stride through the doors of a restaurant like Eastwood parting the double doors of a saloon. My uncle Joe even confused my Eastwood impersonation for another Hollywood star. When I gruffly mumbled a response to some question, Joe said that I only spoke in one-word answers like Gary Cooper.

On those early fly fishing trips, I also learned from legendary guides. Guides who had spent their lives on the Big Hole. They were perfectionists on the river. If they rigged up my line with a certain fly pattern, they wanted it to work. They were the ones who patiently taught me the proper way to cast a fly rod. It also takes grit and determination to be a fly fishing guide. You need a stoic mindset to row a drift boat down a river every day concentrating only on the path of the boat and how someone else is fishing. Much of the stoic aspect of fly fishing can be learned by mimicking how experienced fly fishing guides act on the river.

I also started to see fly fishing as a meditative practice during those summer trips. Throughout the years of religion class and mandatory church attendance at Catholic schools, I learned a prayer that I always liked – the *Serenity Prayer*. For some reason the passage: "God, grant me the serenity to accept things I cannot change, the courage to change things I can, and the wisdom to know the difference," would pop into my head when I was fishing. Perhaps it was a way of soothing my nerves after long stretches of not catching anything. But reciting that prayer as I floated down the river reminded me of the stoic principle that I only have control over certain things in life. Looking up at the big sky and the vast world in the valley surrounding me as I floated down the river, I was also reminded that I am only a small part of an infinite universe.

SIX

RAMMY CACKED!

In the summer of 1992, my grandfather and grandmother, who we called Nonny, bought a cabin on the south end of Flathead Lake on a little peninsula called Finley Point.

To get to the house, you had to drive up a hill on a gravel road with a treacherous blind corner. Once on top of the hill, a dirt road led to the house perched on a cliff in the woods. Although the house was not on the lake, it did have a majestic view looking north-ward up the lake. To the right stood the rolling Mission Mountains, and, to the left, there was the nearly uninhabited Wild Horse Island. On a clear night, you could see the lights of Whitefish Mountain almost a hundred miles north.

Dad had spent a few summer vacations on Flathead Lake as a kid in the 1950s. Nonny's brother, Bill, ran a construction company in Butte and owned a home on the south end of the lake across from Finley Point. On occasions, dad's family would spend a week or two on the lake at Bill's place. Bill had a speed boat and he would spin around the lake and take turns with someone water skiing off the back. Bill was rail-thin and had perfected the art of water skiing on one ski while holding onto the rope in one hand and a cigarette in the other.

Once we had a place to go, my family would make the long trip from New Jersey to Montana each summer. I remember lugging bags through the airport and running to gates to catch our flights. More than once, our connection was cancelled and we had to spend the night in Salt Lake City or Denver. Once we arrived in Montana, dad would rent a car from a place called Rent-a-Wreck and we would cruise up to the lake in a car stuffed with kids and bags.

The lake was an idyllic place for a summer vacation. We would swim and hike and eat huckleberry pie. At night, we would play gin rummy with my grandfather and our uncle Joe Casne, who had married Nonny's sister, Stella. If Joe ever lost a hand of gin rummy, he would use odd phrases like, "I was rammy cacked!" to express his disappointment.

Joe bore a striking resemblance to Rocky Balboa's trainer, Mick, and he had the same type of tough persona. When he was a boy, Joe's father had abandoned his family and moved to Alaska to prospect for gold. Because they were so poor, Joe and his brothers had to live in an orphanage in Twin Bridges, Montana until they were old enough to work. The brothers found jobs in grade school and finally pooled enough money to rent a small apartment in Butte. After high school, Joe fought in World War II and, when he returned to Butte, started his own bar called Casne's Grog Shop.

Joe was also missing the tops of some of his fingers on his right hand. One day while he was grinding meat at the bar to make sandwiches, he got his fingers caught in the grinder. When someone asked what happened after that, Joe would say that he served his customers knuckle sandwiches.

Joe loved to golf and I played golf with Joe many times. If he ever hit a bad shot, he would drop a ball through the hole in his pants pocket and hit another one. Growing up in Butte, Joe knew Bobby Knievel, otherwise known as Evel Knievel. Joe said that he once played the local municipal course in Anaconda when Knievel hit a drive into the fairway of the hole that Joe was playing. Knievel played right through Joe's hole. When Knievel drove by, Joe yelled at him: "Bobby you were a jerk when you were a kid, you were a jerk when you were jumping, and you're still a jerk!"

Joe kept everything he owned immaculately clean, probably because he was never given anything in life. After my sophomore year in high school, he flew out to New Jersey to help me drive our old station wagon to Montana. Joe spent a full day washing the car and vacuuming it out so that it was spotless. All I can remember about that trip was driving through South Dakota and trying to see Mount Rushmore for the first time. On the winding road through the Black Hills, Joe pointed to Mount Rushmore in the distance. When I said I that could see it, that was good enough for him and we kept driving.

Joe and my grandfather had fished together many times since Joe became a part of the family. He could hold the reel and fly line with the nubs of his fingers. One summer, Joe joined us on a fishing trip near Butte. Early in the morning, we stopped by a breakfast place in Whitehall on our way to the Beaverhead River. Joe ordered a cup of coffee with his breakfast. When the waitress brought the cup out, Joe noticed that she kept her thumb dipped in his coffee. When he ordered another cup, he noticed that she did it again. Finally, when he ordered his last cup, he told the waitress to bring it out but without her thumb in it. The waitress said that she only kept her thumb in the cup because she had arthritis and the heat helped numb the pain. Not pleased with her answer, Joe sarcastically told her, "Well, why don't you stick it up your butt if you want to keep it warm?" The waitress replied, "I do in between trips."

One of those first summers at the lake, dad, my grandfather, and Joe planned a short excursion to fish a creek off the Clark Fork River near Missoula. Since it would take over an hour to get to our spot, we loaded up the brown rental station wagon at dawn with our fishing gear and hit the road.

Along the way, we stopped at a grocery store in Arlee and picked up supplies. We packed a bucket of fried chicken, beers, soda, and ice into a foam cooler and got back on the highway. Nothing tastes better after a full morning of fishing than some fried chicken washed down with a beer or soda. My grandfather also picked up a small bottle of whiskey that he stashed away for safe keeping.

At the fishing access site, dad's plan was to try to keep everyone together so that we were all in eyesight in case anything happened. My grandfather and Joe took offense to the idea that they needed anyone to look after them. They were both in their seventies and hated jokes about losing their eyesight or anyone taking away the keys to their cars. So while dad and I walked downriver, they decided to go upriver on their own. For some reason, Joe had a spinning rod in his hand instead of a fly rod. At the end of the line on the rod was a shiny barbed hook.

When we started fishing, it was difficult for me to get my footing in the strong current, and my fly-casting skills had not advanced to the stage to make me a competent fly fisherman. I struggled to find the right spot to fish and get the casts where they needed to go. Dad, however, methodically read the right spots to fish and was able to reel in some good-sized trout at the start of the day.

After a morning of fishing, dad and I trekked back to the car to eat lunch. When I grabbed a chicken breast and a can of soda from the cooler, I noticed that the whiskey bottle in the brown bag was missing. My grandfather or Joe must have snuck away with it.

After lunch, we found a new spot to fish on the creek. Afternoon light poked through the lodgepole pines and sunlight danced along the gentle waves of the stream.

After an hour of fishing, we heard some muffled sounds through the forest brush. It could have been people drinking and horsing around at the access site. But it sounded more serious and we recognized that one of the voices was my grandfather trying to get our attention. We waded out of the river and headed back to the car at the access site.

As we moved through the forest, we could see the figures of two old men standing in the parking lot behind the trunk of our car. It turned out that what my grandfather and Joe said could never happen, did happen. The current was too strong for Joe and he slipped and fell into the river. He flopped around underwater and tried to regain his balance, but he could not stand back up. My grandfather had to rush over to help him out or else he could have drowned. In the commotion, Joe had gotten the hooks and line knotted up around him.

When dad and I approached, we could see that three of the hooks were impaled deep in his hand between his thumb and fingers. For a few moments, Joe stood immobilized until my grandfather told him: "You gotta pull 'em out, Joe!" Joe handed my grandfather his knife and told him to cut the hooks out of his hand. While my grandfather moved the knife closer, Joe turned and thought better of having my grandfather cut them out because, as Joe later explained, my grandfather "was no damn surgeon." Cursing at the sky, Joe yanked the hooks out of his skin, which caused blood to pool and drip off his arm. We used some extra clothes to wipe off the blood, but my grandfather and Joe were concerned about an infection and what that could do. For a few minutes, they discussed what they could use as an antiseptic to clean out the wound. My grandfather then reached into his pants pocket and pulled out the missing bottle of whiskey. He poured whiskey over Joe's arm and hand as Joe winced in pain. They finally bandaged him up with the torn off part of an old shirt.

Joe and my grandfather did not say what caused Joe to slip and fall into the river. Maybe the current was that strong or perhaps he accidentally slipped. I do have a hard time believing that things could have gotten so tangled up without a little assistance from the bottle of whiskey.

Once Joe was all patched up, we got back into the car and drove up to the lake. My grandfather and Joe mostly sat silent on the drive back home. The wounds were clearly more than skin-deep.

SEVEN

MASTERING THE ART OF FLY FISHING

A tributary of the Clark Fork, Rock Creek, is an ideal fly fishing destination. The creek is nestled between tall lodgepole pines,
and it winds through a narrow valley. The only drawbacks are its
slippery floor and hard current.

Early one summer morning, dad and I left the lake and traveled
down I-90 past Missoula to the exit for Rock Creek. We had tak-
en that exit a few times throughout the years to eat at Ekstrom's
Stage Station. My grandfather and Nonny loved Ekstrom's because
it served some of the best huckleberry pie in the state. After Ekstrom's, the paved road turned into a dirt road. The dirt road huddled against a rocky mountain ledge on one side and the tree-lined

bank of the creek on the other. If you met a car coming the other way, it would be difficult to find room to maneuver. And, if you had to pull over on the creek side, you prayed that your car would not tip over the edge.

We drove down the dirt road a few miles and found a spot with enough room to pull off and get our rods rigged up. After getting out of the car, I saw that dirt and dust had caked the sides and back of our car. Dad popped open the trunk and we got our fishing gear out. We next discussed where to fish. I was 16 years old and no longer needed to fish by my dad's side. I could find a spot of my own farther upstream.

We were in the peak of hot summer days in Montana. I wore a t-shirt, shorts, and flip-flops. After following a dirt path through the forest, I traversed down a ledge to the river with my rod in hand. I hopped from one rock to the next on the bank and waded out slightly enough into the river. I knew that I could find fish not only along the banks but also in the water that twisted around the rocks in the center of the creek.

As I steadied myself, I lifted my rod tip up and back with more confidence than any time before. As the line unfurled behind me, I shot the rod in front of me with a strengthened resolve. The fly landed precisely where I wanted it to – slightly above where the fast water met the riffle. The fly caught the slow water and gradually drifted along the riffle before it petered out.

I casted over and over into that section of the river. Things started to feel effortless. I scanned the water surface for the right spots to place the fly. I next hit my mark with the fly as if I were gently reaching out and placing it exactly where I wanted it to go. With enough skill, it felt like each stretch of river opened what was previously concealed.

Once I found a good hole to fish, I sent out shorter casts first to cover the part of the water closest to me. I had learned that reading the water was one of the most important skills in fly fishing. Watching the colorful fly glide over the water, I continued to cast out a little farther each time. And if I did not catch anything, I would cast into a different section of the water.

Fish will seek out the slower current where bugs might drift on top or larvae on the bottom. The fish can spot movement on their periphery. My strategy was not to spook them. The more creases upstream I could find where the fish would be looking up, the more I maximized my chances of catching a fish.

Through the morning and into the early afternoon, I had command of my ability to fly fish like never before. I eventually found a spot on the far bank of the creek where branches from bushes formed a canopy over a stretch of water.

I stood in a focused posture and did my best to mimic Paul Maclean in *A River Runs Through It*. After a couple good casts, I saw the water splash near my line and heard the rip of the line taking off from my reel. Owing to the strong current, the trout in Rock Creek fight hard. And the fish on my line was no exception. It swallowed my nymph and darted headlong upriver looking for underwater branches that it could use to tangle my line and break it off.

I let the fish run while I reeled in all the loose neon line that drifted next to me. Like all the guides taught me, I kept my rod tip high and line tight. The more the fish fought, the more the muscles in my arms and back ached. As the struggle continued, signals alerted my brain that I was in a fight or flight moment and my heart started to pound in my chest. I knew that I had to land that fish.

The fish pulled and darted, ripping my line through the water as I held on. Seconds of time ticked off until the fish finally started to lose its steam. I slowly moved my rod side-to-side and reeled in the line until I saw below me in the water a beautiful rainbow trout with a coat of dark black spots and a streak of red across its belly.

I wetted my hands and picked the big fellow out of the water. I pulled the hook out of its lip. I placed the trout in the creek so that it could swim back to the depths of the river. A shiver of excitement rushed through me. That was the first time I caught a big rainbow on my own. I lifted the bill of my hat, wiped the sweat off my brow, and gazed up the creek.

Believing that more fish could be caught, I casted back into another pool of water, not as a novice, but as someone who knew what he was doing. I next worked my way upstream, covering about a mile or so of the river, and found more riffles to fish. Even though the pounding current tired my muscles, I was happy. I had maneuvered all over the river without another fly fisherman in sight and caught ten good-sized brown and rainbow trout.

Once out of the river, I climbed up the rocky bank of the creek and trudged back through the forest to the little alcove where we parked. I met up with dad and let him know about my success.

In that experience, I finally mastered the art of fly fishing. I knew what was under my control and could connect how everything worked together. I no longer needed to consciously think about how to cast the fly rod. The fly automatically went to the spot I wanted it to go. The movement of the water slowed down and patterns emerged. I could carefully read the water and sense where the trout might be.

The benefit of fly fishing is the affirmation you receive when the line tightens and a trout is on the other end. In that moment, you know that you did things right.

On the river that day, I felt the affirmation of doing things the right way. My nerves calmed, and my mind relaxed. I became more attuned to traces of movement and sound in the world around me. I sensed a spirit or force that moved through the experience. The phenomenon of catching the rainbow trout on my own and being fully immersed in nature felt sublime.

EIGHT

TIME SLIPS AWAY

During the winter of my senior year in high school, my dad received another call from my grandfather with bad news. Uncle Joe was not feeling well. He had cancer and not much longer to live. At the time, Joe lived alone in one of the apartments in the Butte Manor. We decided that it would be good to give him a call. A few days later, dad set up a phone call for me and my sisters and brother so that we could tell Joe how much we loved him. It was not long thereafter that he died.

Dad flew out to Butte for Joe's funeral. Joe did not have a lot of money or many possessions. But when my dad came back, he had an envelope with a few of Joe's things in it. Joe had picked out one or two things to pass on to each of us. He included a little note saying why he had given us each possession. Joe gave me his silver watch. It was no ordinary watch. It had a large case and a stainless-steel band that was a little too large for Joe's wrist. But the silver of the watch matched the silver strands of Joe's hair. Joe had worked as a pit boss at one of the casinos in Las Vegas for a few years. I can imagine him shuffling a deck of cards with the silver watch on one hand and his missing fingers on the other. I still have the watch.

In the spring of my senior year of high school, I also received a letter that I had been waiting a long time to receive. I had worked hard in high school to get into one school, Notre Dame. I applied regular admission and, one day when I came home, a large envelope with Notre Dame's address on it sat on the dining room table. A thick envelope was a good sign, it meant it was likely full of admissions materials. For a moment, the envelope sat in the middle of table staring back at me. When I opened it and learned that I had been accepted, both relief and elation rushed through me. My life had changed.

Time can feel like it stopped or time can feel like it lasts forever. Eventually time slips away. I was fortunate to learn on the river that, in life, some things you can control and some things you cannot. Joe had no control over the fact that he was abandoned as a child and raised in an orphanage, but he made the best of his life. And we could not control that Joe got cancer, but we could choose to reach to him to show we cared.

NINE

LAWS OF EXTRACTION

I spent a couple weeks on Flathead Lake during the summer before college. Feeling the itch to get on the river, dad and my grandfather set up a trip for us to fish the Kootenai River near Libby, Montana.

Libby is about a two-and-a-half-hour drive from the lake. We drove up the westside of the lake and headed northwest. We did not pass many other cars on the way. The farther north we drove, the taller and thicker the lodgepole pines got. If you looked up, all you could see was the vast treetop canopy blocking out the blue sky.

After driving through the early morning hours, we finally reached a fly shop in Libby. I knew a little bit about Libby's troubles. W.R. Grace and Company had owned a large vermiculite mine near town and employed many of the townspeople. Taking pride in the work of the community, the town extolled the use of vermiculite in any conceivable way. The track at the local high school was paved with vermiculite. Gravel pathways in town were sprinkled with it. Vermiculite was used as topsoil in gardens. And all new home and building construction used vermiculite in the siding. It soon turned out that the vermiculite mined outside Libby contained asbestos. Even inhaling one small fiber of asbestos can scar your lungs and cause mesothelioma – a deadly form of cancer.

The history of Libby is similar to Butte's. A dramatic rise in fortune in the beginning followed by a tragic turn and slow decline. What starts out as romance, ends in tragedy. Romantic stories have certain laws of attraction that they follow. Boy meets girl, boy loses girl, and finally boy wins girl back. In the end, the boy wins and everyone is happy. Places like Butte and Libby instead have the laws of extraction. A town's fortune rises, the town collapses, and finally everyone forgets the town. The town loses in the end and no one else cares.

When we stopped in Libby, it was a forgotten place. No one walked the streets downtown. Stores were shuttered. Seats were empty at the restaurants.

In the fly shop, dad asked the guide how things were going in town. The guide said that the people that he knew were not doing well. Many had asbestos in their lungs. At first, the people who got sick were older, mainly in their 60s and 70s, but recently, it was people in their 50s, 40s and sometimes 30s who were getting sick. People's futures were being wiped out in front of their eyes.

We left the fly shop and drove to the dam at the Kootenai River. After getting our rods and gear together, my grandfather staked out a spot near the dam. The water was deeper at that spot, he said. Dad and I left my grandfather to his spot and walked about a mile down the river.

The Kootenai is a wide and strong river, and its water stays cold.

We casted out and scanned the cold water for jumping fish, but the fishing was slow in our section of the river. We did manage to catch a couple small trout, but even that was a struggle. By mid-day, dark clouds formed over our heads and tiny rain drops began to fall.

We then walked back upriver to find my grandfather. He was fishing near the same spot along the rocky shore of the river. We watched him cast as we approached. He had not lost his touch. He was an expert fisherman who was a force of nature with a rod in his hand. He carefully pulled the fly out of the water with little wasted motion, bent his elbow slightly enough to yank the fly line back and rocketed it forward in a quick motion. He kept a smile on his face during the process.

Climbing over and around large boulders on the shoreline, we finally reached my grandfather's spot. Dad twisted his neck to the side so he could look back downriver at the dark clouds gathering directly above.

Dad mentioned to my grandfather that it was unlikely the rain would let up. My grandfather shooed him off, pleading for more time to fish. He was not bothered by some rain. He normally would not take his chances with lighting close by. At least, he taught us never to be on the river with a rod in hand in the middle of thunderstorm. It is better to find a spot to hide until the storm passed. But that day, he decided that he would not go in until the thunder and lightning got closer. Until then, he dutifully kept casting out into the same water.

Dad climbed back over the rocks and tried to find a spot to fish. No one else was foolish enough to still be out on the river. It was too cold and rainy to catch anything.

In the now pouring rain, dad once more called to my grandfather. He broke down his rod and traversed over a few large rocks to make it to the tree-covered edge of the river where we stood and looked out at him.

With the thunderstorm closing in, my grandfather casted out

once more. When he cast, the line slowly suspended in mid-air until it landed on the water surface. As the fly drifted along the water, a dark force from the depths of the river emerged and tugged the fly down. My grandfather's rod bent down to its breaking point. He leaned far back and pointed the rod towards the dark clouds above. After struggling back-and-forth and pulling the line ever closer, he kneeled towards the water and grabbed ahold of a thick brown trout with a white belly thrashing below him. He quickly removed the hook and let him go.

My grandfather had managed to catch a big trout at the last opportunity. The next moment, we heard a large boom like bars of steel colliding above us and saw cracks of lightning in the distance.

After letting the brown trout go, my grandfather tucked his rod under his shoulder and forged a path back to the car. My teeth chattered without me being able to stop them as I watched him walk back with the rain pouring over his hat and raincoat.

In the downpour, we packed up our gear and threw our soaking rain jackets in the truck over all the gear.

The car was warm inside and it buoyed our spirits. The first thing my grandfather did was boast about how many fish he caught. Five or six huge brown trout, he said. He had not caught anything like that for years and they all fought hard. He knew that the big fish were in the deep waters by the dam and he was right.

I believe that was the last time we fished together with my grandfather.

A few years after our trip on the Kootenai, he started to feel poorly and went in for a doctor's appointment before Christmas. After a few tests, the doctor diagnosed him with pancreatic cancer. And it had spread to other parts of his body.

After receiving the news, we traveled to Bethesda, Maryland to spend Christmas with him. I remember my grandfather sitting in a chair in the porch area of his house adjacent to the kitchen. His face looked gaunt. His neck was thinner. His movements were slow, but not his mind. He kept reading. One morning, I saw him in the hallway holding in his lap a copy of Robert Caro's *Master of the Senate* book, which is a profile of Lyndon Johnson's time as Senate Majority Leader. I asked him what he thought of it. He said he liked it because he knew all the characters.

My grandfather died a few months later, but that was only because his body failed. Before we left, he talked about flying out to Seattle after Christmas for a meeting and thereafter visiting an old friend. They had planned to go to a restaurant known for its Alaskan King Crab legs. While telling the story, he mimicked picking up a giant crab leg and taking a big bite out of it. As he did, the edges of his eyes wrinkled with a smile.

TEN

FIVE BELOW

After college, I attended Notre Dame Law School and moved back to New Jersey after graduation. I returned to New Jersey a few years after the September 11th attacks, and the New York City area was continuing to recover. During those years, I worked several jobs, met great friends, and survived both a great recession and once-in-a-lifetime superstorm. New Jersey would likely be where I would build my career and hopefully start a family. But I felt that I had time for some adventure in life. So I started a new job as an Assistant U.S. Attorney in Billings, Montana in 2013.

In Montana, I traded in stock market collapses and super storms for another obstacle – bitter cold winters. In January, I landed at the Billings Airport around midnight and grabbed my two duffel bags at baggage claim. After paying for a rental car, I stepped outside with a bag in each hand. Frigid wind smacked my face. The temperature was around -5 degrees. It felt even colder. I trudged to my rental car fighting against snow, wind, and darkness, and threw my bags inside. As I drove down the steep hill to downtown Billings, I pondered whether this was a new beginning or an end.

I checked into my room at the Dude Rancher Lodge, opened the window a crack, and let the cold Montana air waft in before I fell asleep. Someone had been killed in the lobby of the hotel a year before. But someone else was killed that same week at the other hotel where I was initially going to stay. So I thought I was a step ahead.

Montana winters are not only cold, they are also long. I eventually moved into an apartment in downtown Billings. Staring out my window on the fifth floor, I could see the wind whip snow up from the accumulated piles on the sides of sidewalks and parking lots. One or two intrepid cars slowly glided up the street nearby. I heard the faint whistling sound of the wind canvassing through the levels of a parking garage a block away. To deal with the cold, I bought a big puffy jacket and wrapped a scarf so high around my face that only my eyes peaked out.

But March turned into April, and April into May. The snow and ice receded. Daylight lasted longer. The temperatures rose into the 40s and 50s and suddenly spring had arrived.

After spring runoff, I decided that it was time to try some fly fishing. I had brought my Powell fly rod with me when I moved to Montana. It was the same fly rod that my dad had given to me as a teenager. My next step was to find a fly shop where I could pick up some advice from the locals on where to fish.

I had a couple options to choose from, but I decided to first check out the East Rosebud Fly Shop on the west end of Billings. When I walked through the doors, I heard the booming guitar intro to AC/DC's *Back in Black*. The shop was unique. The owner greeted me when I walked in and I noticed a tattoo of a flopping trout rising up his neck. I next noticed that the store logo was a picture of Angus Young slamming a trout in his arms instead of a guitar. The owner had an exuberant presence. He provided me with some information on fishing near Billings, including on the section of Rock Creek that flows from Billings to Red Lodge, which is a different Rock Creek than the one near Missoula. I then picked out some flies, snagged a new pair of stream boots, and headed out.

The next morning, I woke up before sunrise and packed my car with all the fishing gear. I had bought a new SUV when I moved to Billings because I thought that was what people drove in Montana. I was wrong. People drove pickup trucks. Almost everyone did. Parking lots and city streets were lined with them.

On my way out of town, I drove past chain stores and restaurants on King Avenue and connected onto I-90 west. I took the exit to the highway to Red Lodge and held my breath as the sulphury smell of the refinery seeped through the air vents.

Red Lodge is a hidden ski town with a few blocks of dive bars, knick-knack stores, restaurants, and a great art gallery. The road to Red Lodge is dotted with fishing access sites for the creek that runs parallel with the road.

I picked the fishing access site before town and parked in a deserted parking lot. To get to the creek, I had to gingerly climb down a steep, rocky hill and hang onto tree branches along the way. After my descent, I walked to the creek and started casting into the water. Stepping into the creek felt like entering both a new and old world. New for me because I was now a Montana resident myself. But it was also like stepping into the old world inhabited by my grandfather and dad when they fished in Montana decades before.

As runoff had recently ended, the water continued to move fast and crested over some rocks in the middle of the creek, but I was still able to get a good drift with my fly. The high water level also created enough room below the water surface for trout to maneuver in deep pockets.

By mid-morning, I found a perfect fishing hole. Water poured over a gravel bar into a long turn that created a confluence of fast and slow water. I casted into the crease created by the clash of the two currents and instantly felt a hit on the line. Pulling my rod closer, I reached down to find a nice rainbow. I gently pulled out the hook and released it back into the water. I soon caught a colorfully spotted brook trout and then another one.

As I worked my way up the creek, I caught a couple more trout. Within a half hour, I had already reeled in five. Branches and leaves hung over the creek creating a canopy. Splinters of sunlight shone through the leaves. I did not want my fishing adventure to end. Farther up, a tall tree had fallen over the creek. I extended one leg and the next over it so I could continue upriver.

As I pushed forward, the creek widened out. Turned up tree stumps, remnants of spring runoff, lay fallow on the rocky beaches. Once the thick forest on the edge of the creek thinned out, I could see wide-open ranchland with horses grazing in the fields. I did not encounter another person along the way.

The sun remained perched high in the sky when I decided to call it a day. I had been fishing since early morning and had caught twelve fish. When I stepped out of the creek, I could feel the stress of moving to a new city wash away.

ELEVEN

ADVENTURES IN PONY

In early 2015, a friend from college texted with an idea. Since I lived in Montana, we should plan a summer fly fishing trip for our group of friends. In a long response, I wrote out a proposed itinerary and eventually the plan came together.

To begin the trip, we fished for two straight days in July on the Big Hole River during the scorching hot part of summer. Between the first and second days of fishing, we stopped for dinner at Lydia's, one of the last remaining Italian supper clubs in Butte. At a supper club, every course comes with your meal. After a long day on the river, we gulped down whiskeys and ordered unlimited amounts of raviolis, spaghetti, and fries to go with our dinner steaks.

After two successful days of fishing on the Big Hole, we next drove down a rocky road that led to Twin Bridges and from that point we drove on to Virginia City.

In Virginia City, we stopped for drinks at the Bale of Hay Saloon and paid our respects to the ghost of Thomas Meagher. The saloon had a large wooden bar and stacks of alcohol packed high behind it. Not far away from the saloon, the first vigilantes of Virginia City had hung the road agents and affixed the 3-7-77 sign on them as a warning.

After drinks in Virginia City, we ate dinner at the Gravel Bar in Ennis. At dinner, we were so tired from fishing that our limbs sagged and eyelids had to be forcefully kept open. But a good country western band and a few shots of whiskey kept us at the bar later than we probably needed to be.

When we woke up the next morning to fish the Madison River, we found that smoke from forest fires had blown in through the night. The smoke blocked out the horizon and anything within a ten-to-twenty foot distance of where we stood. Once on the drift boats, all we could see was the water in front of us and the first yard of tall grass on the banks. Maybe it would have been better to play golf that day. But we nonetheless capped off our inaugural fly fishing trip by catching a few fish.

From that trip forward, we have tried to gather back in Montana each summer for a yearly fly fishing trip. It may not work out every summer, but we have had more adventures over the years.

During one trip, we headed to Pony, Montana and sauntered into the Pony Bar on our last night. Walking into the bar, I saw a signed photograph on the back wall of a cowboy on a bucking horse at a rodeo. I noticed that the cowboy on the horse was Rooster Reynolds, the guide who had taken my dad and I up on horseback into the Pintler Mountains twenty years before. It was good to see that Roster had earned some respect.

It had been a rough day of fishing on the Jefferson. The water was muddy and we had not had much luck. A few drinks at the Pony Bar were supposed to be our reward.

We sat at a table by the bar and recapped the day. A bald drunkard kept glancing at us with a malevolent look. He looked to be in his late forties and sat at the bar alone. He wore just a white t-shirt and a pair of jeans. He had ordered a tall glass of whiskey neat moments before and told the bartender that he gets mean when he drinks whiskey.

He did not plan to take us all on by himself. In between drinks, he would walk over to the local guys playing pool on the other side of the bar. While he spoke to them, they would all look over at us. He probably told them that we kept looking over at them and laughing. In reality, we were minding our own business. But it does not take much to get the local guys at a bar riled up for a fight. It is practically a sport in Montana.

As the bald drunkard walked over to the guys playing pool and whispered in one's ear, the lights in his eyes grew dimmer. After talking to the local guys, he would stagger back to his seat at the bar. He then suddenly slammed down his drink and wandered over to our table. He slurred something about us laughing at the guys by the pool table all night. When I disputed his account, he said: "Oh, I'm taking you out first!" I stood up and showed him that I was about a foot taller. He backed away for the moment.

We did not want to return to our jobs on Monday with black eyes and busted teeth. To try to quell the tension, one of my friends walked out of the bar to talk with a couple of the local guys who had been playing pool. He said to come get him if he was not back in five minutes. After a few minutes passed, my friend came back into the bar and warned us that it was time to leave.

We finished our drinks and paid our tab without any sight of the pool players. But as we turned the corner outside the bar, we saw a black pickup truck pull up. The doors opened and sets of cowboy boots dropped to the ground. The reinforcements had arrived and they were ready for a fight. We were clearly outnumbered, but we did not have time to stick around to see who was getting out or what weapons they may have been holding on to.

Without wasting time, we jumped into our truck and I started the engine. As I turned onto the road behind the bar, I looked back to confirm that the black pickup was not behind us. I hit the gas and booked it down the deserted road into the pitch-black night. As I drove, I kept checking the mirror every few seconds to make sure that we were not being followed.

It took a half hour to make it back to our hotel in Three Forks. We were tired and missed out on enjoying drinks at the bar to end our trip. But the Pony Bar is no place for out-of-towners to get into a fight.

TWELVE

THIS AIN'T TEXAS

In June 2016, I decided to spend a weekend in Butte to fish the Big Hole. I thought that I could catch a fish and grill it for dinner. I had it all planned out. I checked the limit on how many fish you could keep on the Big Hole. I went to the local sports store in town and bought a knife and a little grill. I had a plate and fork packed away.

Cooking a fish for dinner is a natural thing to do. People have been catching fish for food on rivers for centuries. It would be an authentic experience, I thought. And it would take me back to the first time that I fished when my grandfather pulled out a knife and showed me how to cut open a trout.

When I got to the river, I found a good spot at a fishing access site near Melrose that also had a camp site.

I worked my way upstream and waded out so that I could get a few good drifts in the riffles that formed past rocks. Soon enough, I caught a good-sized brown trout. I stayed in the same section and casted out farther. Within a half hour, I caught three similar-sized browns.

Even though I planned to catch a fish to cook, I could not do it. Those brown trout were too nice to keep and eat. They belonged in the river. So each time I caught a fish, I tossed it back into the river where it belonged.

After catching a few fish, I walked upriver to find another good spot to fish. I saw a small island in the distance and a section where the river had reconnected after the end of the island. But the water was too high and fast to be able to wade out to the good spot. After a couple hours, I decided to call it a day and head back to my truck.

While packing up my gear, a man climbed out of the RV next to my truck. He was thin with scraggly hair and had on a tank top. He looked to be in his 50s. Squinting in the sun, he looked me over and asked how the fishing was. I said it was pretty good. I caught a few.

He next asked where I was from. I told him I lived in Billings, but my dad's side of the family was from Butte. He said he was from Butte too. He asked my last name and I told him – McCarthy. He said, "I knew it!" and proceeded to list all the people he knew with McCarthy names in Butte. He ticked off a few names, thought for a moment, and named a few more. I smiled and said that I did not know any of them, but, if you go back long enough, we were all probably connected.

It was a friendly conversation up to that point, but he then he sternly said:

"Butte just ain't the same no more."

I knew that to be true, but I was curious as to what he meant.

"What do you mean?" I asked.

He said, "It's all these dang foreigners moving in."

At that point, I wanted to leave the conversation, but my gear was not packed up and it would have been rude to leave. Out of curiosity, I asked him where the foreigners were from.

"Texas!" he exclaimed.

Given the possibilities, I was relieved that Texas was the answer.

Curiosity got the best of me again, so I asked another question.

"And what are they doing?"

He started to unload his thought, "Oh, well..." he paused and continued, "they moved out here last year and ran for city council and won. Now they have also these new-fangled ideas." The emphasis was on *new-fangled*, as if that word justified his frustrations.

He continued, "They want to put in bike paths and parking spots that are like sideways, not the regular way, you know."

With his hands, he showed me how the parking spots would be slanted at an angle and not parallel to the sidewalk.

"Well, I suppose that would save room for parking," I said.

He was not pleased with my response.

"They can take their ideas back to Texas!" he said emphatically.

He then climbed back into the RV and slammed the door. I drove away thinking that only in America could someone be in one of the most scenic settings in nature and be upset about something as mundane as parking spots.

THIRTEEN

MEET THE GOVERNOR

During my first few summers in Montana, I would meet my dad for a short fly fishing trip. We mostly fished the Big Hole River, but one summer dad was invited to fish with a couple friends on the Missouri River north of Helena. Dad needed another fisherman on his boat and he invited me to join.

After staying in Helena for the night, we planned to meet dad's friends in the morning at the fly shop in the little town of Craig that sits right along the river. On the drive north from Helena, we ascended Highway 15 and passed by Prickly Pear Creek. We next passed by Wolf Creek, which is a narrow creek that runs along the highway. Thereafter, we drove past the signs for Holter Lake and the Big Belt Mountains. The Big Belts are a range of rigid-peaked mountains with a smattering of pine trees on its grass-covered slopes. As we ascended upward, a vista opened to the wide and winding Missouri River. I saw that the river splits in sections like a delta. As the river shoots off in different directions, small islands formed in between the current.

We drove into town in the early morning light. Craig has a couple fly shops, a restaurant, and some lodging. At the end of the road through town is a sign for Izaak's, a restaurant named after the English angler Izaak Walton. A sign outside said that it offers "Fresh Food, Spirits, and Gambling." I am not sure what Sir Izaak would think about the spirits and gambling part.

The fly shop in Craig is a log cabin with brown siding and a long porch in the front. One sign on the side of the shop said "Spend More Time on the River." Next to it, a sign indicated that this is "Fly Fishing Headquarters." When the fishing is good, the Missouri may well be the headquarters for fishing in Montana. That morning the fly shop was buzzing with guides and fisherman ready to get out onto the river. Outside the shop were rows of drift boats and rafts, all waiting to be driven to the put-in spot.

After catching up with dad's friend, dad and I hopped into our guide's truck and headed out of town. Along the way we drove over the Governor Forrest H. Anderson Memorial Bridge, which extends over the banks of the Missouri. Looking upriver, I saw the rugged cliffs that lined each side of the river in certain spots as it winds through the canyon.

Forrest Anderson was the Attorney General of Montana from 1957 to 1969 and the Governor of Montana from 1969 to 1973. As Attorney General, Anderson helped negotiate an end to a riot at the Montana State Prison in Deer Lodge in 1959. The prisoners had taken over the prison at one point. My grandfather was serving as the County Surveyor in Silver Bow County at the time and he was called in the middle of the night to help quash the riot. He grabbed his pistol and drove from Butte to Deer Lodge in the night. But the riot had fortunately ended by the time he got to the state prison.

My grandfather knew Forrest Anderson well, they were friends and he helped Anderson on some of his campaigns. My grandfather said that when Anderson was governor, he owned an RV park and bar near the bridge in Craig and he would spend time near the river on the weekends. One weekend in the fall, Anderson was outside of the RV's picking up trash and had on some old clothes. One of the guests at the RV park approached Anderson thinking that he was the local caretaker. The guest asked Anderson about the area and Anderson chatted with him for a little bit. The friendly guest then thanked him and asked if he worked for the property owner. Anderson replied that he did not work for the owner, he was the owner and the Governor of Montana. The guest's mouth dropped as he turned away in disbelief. The guest went into the office at the RV park and told the person at the front desk that the caretaker outside thinks he is the Governor of Montana. The receptionist said, "He is."

As we drove to the canyon section of the Missouri River, we passed by fenced-in pastures with stacks of hay piled high. Cows and sheep grazed on the grass. At the access site, the river was wide and moved slowly over the rocky bottom and sandy bars.

The beginning of July was the perfect time to fish the Missouri River. If we had fished earlier in the year, the water may have been too high. If we fished later, the rocks could have been too mossy, and the moss would have covered our flies.

Our guide had grown up on a big ranch in central Montana, but once he started fly fishing, he was hooked. The two main rivers he fished now were the Bighorn and Missouri. When we first met him, we mentioned that we knew how to fly fish, but he seemed surprised by our proficiency once we were out on the water.

As we floated down the river, our guide rowed steadily back-and-forth to the banks and told us to cast as tightly as possible against the bank. He had set up our rig with double nymphs and a bobber with a little weight. That allowed the flies to sink down to where the big fish might be feeding. I complied with his instructions and was able to cast my fly an inch or two from the bank without it getting caught in the Cottonwood branches.

I followed my orange bobber as it drifted along the edges of the river. Without warning, the bopper would drop sharply in the water and I would feel a forceful tug like someone was trying to pull my arm out of the socket. My rod would bend sharply and I knew I had to instantly set the hook. If I did not, our guide would be extremely disappointed that I may have let a big one get away and I would hear it from him.

I rarely saw the fish come up to the surface at first strike. Instead, my line would jerk back-and-forth and the fish would dart upriver, downriver, or under the boat. The fish in the Missouri were big and fought hard. Throughout the day, dad and I caught almost twenty big browns and rainbows. Sometimes we had a fish on both our lines at the same time. The rainbows in the Missouri had dark spots on their sides with an almost purplish streak across their body. The browns had a tan and yellow-ish hue beneath their abundance of dark spots.

When we stopped for lunch, dad's friend noticed a boat passing by with people that he recognized. He saw that it was one of his nephews and called out to him. The friend's son was also the guide on the friend's boat. When the nephew came over to greet my dad's friend, a rollicking family reunion with hugs and laughter broke out in the middle of the river.

While we drifted down the river in the afternoon, I asked the guide if he guided for anyone famous recently. A lot of guides will have interesting stories about people who they recently guided. To protect their clients, guides can be careful about what they tell other people, but sometimes the stories are too good not to tell.

Our guide said that he recently guided for a well-known politician. The guide, who grew up far away from the politician's city, said that the politician was a little insulted when the guide did not recognize him. But the guide was a little proud of the fact that he ruffled the politician.

The guide said that the biggest fish the politician caught that day was a whitefish over twenty-inches. Whitefish have a small, circular mouth that look like the mouth of a sucker fish. Some fly fishermen in Montana perceive whitefish as bottom feeders. They do not even think that whitefish count as a catch. Others know that whitefish are native to Montana and give them their due respect. In any event, the politician was overjoyed by his catch. He thought he had caught the biggest fish in his group for the day. He asked the guide to take a picture of himself with the whitefish, proudly holding it up in his hands. To boast about his prize, he texted his buddies a picture of him with a wide grin holding onto the fish. The guide knew that his friends had been fishing on the Missouri before and would probably lambast him for bragging about catching a whitefish. But the guide kept his mouth shut.

The next day, the guide asked if the politician had dinner the night before. The politician said he arrived for dinner and was ready to be congratulated by everyone for catching the biggest fish. But, instead of congratulations, the politician was met with laughter from his friends. Why didn't you warn me, the politician asked our guide? The guide shrugged his shoulders and kept rowing the boat.

The politician had to learn for himself that no one brags about catching a whitefish in Montana. He was humbled and his friends probably would never let him live it down. In his day job, he may have been used to praise from everyone around him. But, on the Missouri River, he learned that pride comes before the fall.

As a general rule, Montanans do not like braggarts. Like Forest Anderson, it is better to be mistaken for a caretaker at a cabin retreat than the Governor that owns them.

FOURTEEN

SMALL MIRACLES

In the summer of 2018, I had been living in Montana for almost five years, and I had settled into a good life and routine. In the summers, I would meet my dad or friends in Melrose to fish the Big Hole, or I would take a trip to one of the access sites near Billings on the Stillwater or Bighorn.

But then something improbable happened.

In August 2018, I took a short trip to Flathead Lake to visit family. Afterwards, I checked in with my family and learned that my sister had broken her arm. She had remained at the lake for a few weeks during her summer break from teaching. Every day she would go for a run or walk on the road that loops around Finley Point. It is an idyllic place for a run. The seven-mile journey takes you up and down steep hills and through twisting turns in the road. Along the way, a view of the glistening lake peeks through gaps in between branches on the pine trees.

One day after I left, my sister had a fluke accident where she tripped on a branch lying in the road and catapulted toward the ground. When she lunged her arms out to protect herself, she shattered her humerus in several places.

While she was lying on the side of the road, a neighbor saw her and stopped his car. He was able to talk with her to see what was wrong and helped to call my parents. An ambulance came and transported my sister to a hospital in Polson.

The doctor at the hospital said that, given the severity of the break, a good surgeon was needed. My sister could have had the surgery done locally, but my parents decided to see if any top surgeons nearby in the state could help. Dad found a good orthopedic surgeon in Bozeman, who usually operated on injuries for the U.S. Ski Team. The orthopedic surgeon, however, did not have any available appointments for about another week.

My sister waited out the time until her appointment at my parent's cabin at the lake. She spent all day and night sitting in a reclining chair trying to avoid the pain of moving the arm around. Our family dog, Ajax, stayed by her side and carefully watched anyone that came near her.

The day before her appointment with the orthopedic surgeon, dad gently helped my sister into his car and they drove down to Bozeman.

My sister's arm did heal and the surgeon did an excellent job. But the story is about someone else who had been wounded a long time ago and was also looking for a chance to heal.

While waiting in the orthopedic surgeon's office, dad passed the time by checking his cell phone and flipping through the magazines on the table.

He eventually struck up a conversation with another patient. The patient said that she lived in Melrose. She had been out on an ATV and flipped over causing her injury. Dad said that he knew Melrose well. He had grown up in Butte and fished on the Big Hole River many times.

Any other time, the conversation would have been about the places in town like the fly shop or Hitchin' Post Restaurant, or my dad would reminisce about some old fishing stories.

But, at the beginning of the conversation, the young woman said that her dad had once been a fly fishing guide on the Big Hole. Dad asked who that could be. She said that her dad passed away years ago and his name was Phil Smith. Did he know him, she asked?

Dad, of course, said that he knew Phil Smith. Phil was one of the best guides on the river. He guided for us many times over the years, including my first fishing trip.

Phil's daughter said that she was only a young girl when he died. She did not get to know him and they did not have many pictures of him. Since he was a guide, her family tries to see if people had any pictures of him from past trips. She asked my dad if he had any.

Yes, he did. Dad emailed me later that day and asked if I could take a picture of my photo with Phil holding the rainbow trout on the Madison River during my first fly fishing trip. I found the old photo and emailed a copy of it back. With the blink of an eye, the photo found its way to Phil's daughter.

Was this simply a lucky coincidence or a small miracle? For most of my life, I never thought about bringing the picture with me wherever I moved. For twenty-six years, I just happened to bring it along. It was like an old t-shirt that I could not get rid of. But now the picture had a purpose. It provided Phil's daughter with a memory of her father. It was not only a memory of what he looked like, but a memory of him in his best light. A picture that displayed his warmth, kindness, and ability. Perhaps it was a small miracle.

I do not know how Phil's daughter reacted to seeing the picture. Hopefully, she was amazed. But for me, sending a copy of the picture felt like life had come full circle. Phil had handed me the fish on the Madison River, and I sent a picture capturing that moment to his daughter twenty years later. Like a poem, the picture had added another verse to its meaning. Perhaps we instinctively know what memories to keep with us. And the memory will find a way to live on.

FIFTEEN

CHANCE ENCOUNTERS

I met my wife, Samantha, in Big Sky, Montana during a ski trip in early 2017. We lived in different parts of the country, but we continued to see each other about once a month. One month, I would fly out to the East Coast either to see Samantha where she lived in Boston, or to explore cities like Charleston or Savannah. Other months, Samantha would travel out to Montana to see me.

On one of the trips to Montana, Samantha had the courage to go with me to the Bucking Horse Sale in Miles City, Montana – otherwise known as the Mardi Gras of Montana. By day, thousands of people watched a rodeo at the Eastern Montana Fairgrounds. By night, a rollicking block party took over downtown Miles City. During our day at the rodeo, Samantha and I found a seat at the top of one of the bleachers. A young cowboy who probably had too much to drink sat down next to Samantha and got a little too cozy. I wrapped my arm around Samantha and tried to pull her closer. But I soon realized it was not Samantha's arm I was grabbing; it was the young cowboy's arm. The astonished cowboy yelled down the row to his friends: "Hey, this chick's trying to hit on me!" At once, we both realized that it was my hand on his arm and we all awkwardly left the bleachers.

Even after that episode at the Bucking Horse Sale, Samantha nevertheless agreed to continue dating me and we were married in late 2018. Samantha moved to Billings in early 2019. Then the pandemic started in 2020.

The pandemic severely hit some of the more populated parts of Montana. We cautiously followed all the guidance to keep ourselves and people in our community safe. Nevertheless, having to live through a life-threatening pandemic can weigh on your soul. Eventually you need to find a way to break free and de-stress. After surviving the first few months of the pandemic, the summer offered Samantha and I a slight reprieve and chance to unwind.

We used that first summer during the pandemic as an opportunity to see more of Montana. We traveled through Yellowstone National Park and gazed at scattered packs of bison in the Lamar Valley. We drove over and down the perilous Beartooth Pass. We took a trip to Ennis, the fly fishing capital of Montana, and walked along the nearby wood-planked streets of Virginia City. We scaled bumpy roads up to remote lakes in the northwest corner of Glacier National Park.

Before the days got too cold, we planned one more trip, this time to Melrose. In October, trees with vivid yellow, orange, and red leaves lined the river's edge. It was almost like New England in the fall. I made a reservation at the cabins across from the fly shop in Melrose for one of the last weekends of the month, but an early snowstorm swept through the Big Hole Valley the same day and we pushed the trip back.

The next weekend, Sam and I set out from Billings with our dog,

Bo. I first saw Bo's picture on the internet a couple years earlier. I was not seriously looking for a dog, but Bo was a little puppy with floppy ears, whiskers, and sweet brown eyes. He reminded me of our family dog, Ajax, when he was a puppy. On a whim, I contacted the rescue shelter to see if I could meet him. The owner of the shelter said that Bo was rescued from the Northern Cheyenne Reservation and he was found under an abandoned bus with his mother, brother, and sister. At the shelter, Bo's brother and sister tussled on the far side of a gated area. But Bo pressed his check against the fence and looked up at me with his soft brown eyes. I paid the owner a hundred dollars and took him home.

On our trip to Melrose, we left Billings and took the highway that runs next to the meandering Yellowstone River. We drove up the curvy road that crosses the Continental Divide and drops down into Butte. Late into the evening, we finally arrived at the cabin in Melrose.

We had everything we needed in our cabin – a kitchen, television, and heat. The weather was warm during the day, but the temperature plummeted at night. We cracked the windows open and I drifted off to dreams of colorful trout swimming through the cabin like a Monte Dolack painting.

When I woke up, I sauntered over to the fly shop next door and spoke with the one of the owners. He said that business had been slow at first during the pandemic, but it had picked up during the peak weeks. He also warned that a couple people in town had gotten the virus and it was probably better to order takeout if we needed food.

My guide and I hopped into his Toyota truck and we took a right out of the dusty parking lot. On a morning like that, the sun needed time to rise high enough to reach over the mountain tops to warm the river. Consequently, the guide and I were both bundled up in ski hats and gloves and heavy jackets when we first arrived at the river.

No other fishermen were in sight on the river that day. There was not enough sunlight to rouse the fish out of their lethargic state. Only the tiniest fish had the energy to chase after our flies. I caught six fish, mostly rainbows, throughout the day. The guide tried every type of combination of flies to lure the bigger fish to come out, but it did not work.

After fishing, Sam and I took Bo for a walk. We crossed the street that runs through Melrose and, on the other side, stepped over train tracks that may or may not have been in use. We walked past an abandoned hotel and past some of the homes abutting the river. After a while, we decided to drive down to the nearest fishing access site to let Bo run by the river.

When Bo jumped out of the truck, his tongue flopped out of his mouth and drool poured to the ground. He spun and darted toward a sound in the trees, his tail and hair on his back pointed up. As Sam and I followed him, he sniffed around and led us down the beaten path that fishermen use to access the river.

After walking back down the path, Bo ran through the gravel lot to a clearing of grass by the river. Next to the river, I noticed a plaque on the ground. I looked at the name and saw that it was a memorial for Phil Smith.

The plaque indicated that Phil was only 57 years old when he died. It read:

> This plaque is dedicated to honor and remember a true friend and pioneer of the Big Hole River. As a naturalist, sportsman and guide, you touched the lives of many. Your respect and love for the Big Hole River lives on.

The plaque was a little worn out and darkened by the weather. Long blades of green grew near its base. Beyond the plaque, the river flowed under a bridge and downstream in its natural rhythm.

It had been almost thirty years since I had first met Phil. Memories of our first trip flooded into my mind. I recalled standing on the rocky bank as Phil handed me the rod with the rainbow trout on the line and the fear that ran through me like an electric shock. I thought about the picture of Phil and I with the rainbow and hoped that it brought some solace to his daughter. I imagined what it would have been like for a little girl to lose her dad at such an early age.

I also knew that this was the right place for Phil. He spent his life on the river and it was where his spirt belonged. It was a reminder of trying to find peace in a traumatic world.

Fly fishing can be one of the ways to release negative stress and trauma from our body. When we fly fish, we are immersed in nature. Our eyes are used in almost a hypnotic way. The fly rod is released back-and-forth almost like a finger being waved in front of you during hypnosis. You follow the fly along its path in the water, which can put you almost in a deeply meditative trance. If you want to further calm yourself, you can take deep breaths of fresh air into and out of your lungs. The deep breaths help to slow down your heart rate and put you further into a calming state.

Fly fishing is also therapeutic because it puts you in control of your own actions. People who have gone through trauma in their lives can sometimes feel so out of control in certain situations that they become paralyzed by inaction or terrified by fear. That reflects the brain's fight-or-flight mechanism going into hyperdrive.

To get out of the constant loop of fear or paralysis due to trauma, it helps to engage in activities where we feel in control. Once you become good enough at fly fishing, you gain the ability to read the water and know where you must cast the fly. Without even realizing it sometimes, all your actions become both intentional and second-nature. When the line drifts too far, you mend it. When the strike indicator or fly dip into the water, you pull the rod up to set the hook. All the while, you find yourself in a glorious natural setting and in control of your body and actions.

People do not include fly fishing in the categories of practices that help you heal from trauma like meditation or yoga. But they should. Fly fishing has everything those practices have and, even more; you immerse yourself in a beautiful setting while doing it. It is a form of spiritual healing.

SIXTEEN

RITUALS

In the chaotic beginning of the pandemic, some people turned to rituals to make it through each day. Some of those rituals were as simple as going for a run or baking bread. I saw one video of two best friends who walked miles away from their homes each day only to high five and then walk back home.

As the pandemic stretched on, I decided that fly fishing would become my ritual. I would try to fish as much as a could in 2021. I knew a little bit about religious rituals. They can include sacred places. Church or a synagogue would be the most obvious sacred place. In Native American religions, a river or mountain can be a sacred place. A place where a miracle happened can be a sacred place. Or an important battlefield can feel sacred. Once a place is established as sacred, people tend to return to it to relive or grasp the experience. In the repetition of returning to the source, people step out of ordinary time and enter eternal time. Time becomes measured not by the hours on the clock, but by a connection to the past. When you go to a sacred space, you are connected to what happened at that place even if it was decades or centuries ago.

Religious rituals, though, are not restricted to organized religion. Every spring, pitchers and catchers report to spring training camp and the ritual of the baseball season starts anew. Parents bring their children to the same baseball stadiums that their parents brought them to. During the playoffs, fans hope to experience the miraculous moments that captured their imagination in the past. If baseball can be a religious ritual,[10] why not fly fishing?

Moreover, as my grandfather said, the river is like poetry. Poetry can spark the imagination and enliven the spirit. A good poem can be read again to bring back the wonder when it was first read. I thought of my commitment to fly fishing that year as a kind of poetic exegesis. The more I fished, the more I might be able to uncover the rhythm and structure that makes the river like a poem.

The winter that year was long. Snow blanketed the ground for weeks and months on end. The sky was always filled with ominous grey and white puffy clouds ready to dump the next batch of snow. My skin froze every time I walked outside.

Sometime in March, blue sky started to peek out from the clouds. The snow melted into the rivers nearby and the water rose. The trees were barren and the brittle grass was a lifeless yellow above the frozen ground. Soon birds started chirping and the sun began setting later in the day. It felt like spring was on the horizon.

Toward the third week of March, I decided to plan my first trip to the river that season. The weather the week before had started in the mid-40s, rose up into the 50s, and finally dipped back down into the 30s during the weekend. But the extended forecast called for mild days the next week and temperatures reaching up to 50 degrees by the next weekend.

That was enough to get me out of the house and over to the fly shop. I talked with the owner of the fly shop about how the fishing was that time of year. He had already fished Rock Creek and the Stillwater River. He said that with the warmer weather, nice-sized rainbow trout would be making their way down from the upper mountain lakes in the Absarokee Range and into the Stillwater River. I might get lucky and run into a midgefly hatch. He had worked a lot of streamers and, from his reaction, it appeared that he had done well. He said that fish could be caught that time of year with a big bug on top and a small nymph, like a copper john, below it. I picked up some of those flies and, if the weather held up, I would make my way over to the Stillwater on Sunday.

That night I gathered all the fishing equipment that I stored away over the winter. I found my waders and boots. I checked the bag tucked away in my closet where I kept my reels, fishing vest, and other equipment. Before going to bed, I laid them all out on the floor like it was the night before Christmas.

In the morning, I took my time. I figured that the cold water temperatures would keep the fish lethargic in the morning and getting a late start would not impact my chance to catch some fish.

But I could not wait too long. Samantha was seven months pregnant with our first baby and I only had a small window to get out and fish. I backed out of the driveway and waved goodbye to Samantha as I drove away.

After taking the exit for Columbus on the highway, I drove through the small town of Absarokee. Shops, restaurants, a hotel called the Big Yellow House and a few churches lined the main street. I noticed a Suburban driven by a man wearing a brown jacket and tie, and I assumed that he was taking his family to church. It felt like a spiritual day.

I turned right at the intersection in downtown Absarokee and took the road that leads to the Stillwater River. At the first access site, I drove over a bridge with wooden planks that ran perpendicular on the bottom. My tires went clump-clump each time they drove over the space connecting the planks. I wondered how supportive those planks were. Later in the summer, I learned the answer when I returned to that fishing access site and saw that the bridge was closed and had a big chain across it.

At the first access site, the water was too low to be able to fish it. So I decided to leave and drive down to the next access site a few miles away.

At Cliff Swallow access site, I saw that the parking lot was empty, and decided to park. After putting together my rod and reel and tying a girdle bug and small Copper John fly to the end of it, I walked down to the river.

I had sprained my ankle only a few weeks before and had to walk gingerly along the bank. The terrain on the side of the river was rocky and any misstep meant that my ankle could get twisted again. There was ice on the bank and eventually I could not walk any farther. Under Montana law, you can only walk up to the highwater mark. So I climbed up a hill and imagined that the water could have risen as high up as where I was walking through the forest. I walked along that ridge until I came upon a gulley with a level decline that led me back to the river.

From there, the water was so low that what would have been the river was only a field of rocks. I walked over the rocks and found a section where a couple boulders sat in the middle of the river. The water there was deep enough that I could not see to the bottom. As a general rule, if I can see to the bottom of the river then fish are most likely not around.

I walked into the icy water and struggled to keep my balance on the mossy rocks. I was able to find a spot where I could cast into where a foam line formed after one of the boulders. I casted a couple times into that section without any luck and watched as my girdle bug sank each time. Without seeing the girdle bug floating, I would not be able to see any strikes on the nymph. My efforts seemed hopeless that day.

Right as I was about to bring my line in again and put more gunk on the top fly, I felt my line catch something. I thought that the nymph got stuck on a rock or stick and, at first, pointed my rod to where I thought the fly would be to break it off. But suddenly a small silver fin splashed out of the water as my line tightened and a fish darted away from me. I pulled in the extra slack and fought with the fish as it's spotted belly with a pinkish stripe flipped upward.

I crept backwards trying to steady myself on the rocks so that I would have a sturdy place to bring the fish in and take the hook out. I picked up the fish and tried to take the hook out quickly, but it was deep in the fish's mouth and the fish bit down on my finger. I dipped it back into the water so it would not be harmed and tried again before finally gently prying the hook out of the fish's lip. I did not want to hurt the fish. I held it only inches from water level and dropped it back into the water once the hook was out. I felt relieved once its tail waived back and forth and it was able to swim away.

I stayed at that spot a little longer and caught another fish who spit the fly out of its mouth once I brought it in close. I kept fishing that spot for another hour. Time seems slower on a river in winter. I had on a ski hat and could see my breath waft in front of me like steam. I felt my heartbeat soften like the snow on the banks of the river.

During one cast, the nymph got caught on the lace of my boot. When I put my hand in the water for only a few seconds, the frigid water stung so much that I had to take my hand out. I walked upriver looking down on the brownish rocks below trying to find a good spot to plant a foot. But sometimes a rock would tumble away after I set my foot. After one step, I did lose my balance and I quickly moved my arms in front of me to brace for a fall before gathering myself. If I fell into the river, my waders could have swelled up with water and I would have sunk like an anchor.

I casted a few more times into the water and watched my colorless line drop into the ripples. I looked down at how the water shifted from shades of green to deep blue and pulled my fly out again.

After an hour, I walked back along the rocky bank and over the melting ice packs. Along the way, I noticed footprints and paw prints; maybe they were from a dog and another fisherman earlier in the day. I climbed back up the hill that I had traversed down. While trying to walk sideways down the hill, I felt the bottom of my boot slip on the mud and I tumbled on my back down the hill as I held my rod up in the air. I gathered myself again and decided to call it a day.

Although I only caught a couple fish and fell down a hill in the process, it was not a total loss. For a few hours on the cold Stillwater River, I found a way to be still. Still as in a place where I was both free and open to the world around me. Where I was neither moving towards something nor away from something.

SEVENTEEN

FIRE SEASON: PART I

In May, our daughter Bille Grace was born. Pregnancy felt like an eternity, but the moment was finally here. Our world changed when we first saw our daughter's face. We were also surprised by her colorful red hair. After a couple months, we took our Billie Grace up to Flathead Lake to see family.

During the first days at the lake, a cover of white smoke wafted over the Mission Mountains and blurred out the sky. It may have been smoke blowing in from wildfires in California, Oregon, or Washington. Even a little precipitation would have cleared out the clouds. But we were in the middle of one of the worst droughts in the western part of the United States in decades and no rain clouds were in sight.

To try to escape the smoke, dad and I planned a trip down to Melrose to fish the Big Hole River for one day. When we left the lake in the late afternoon, the smoke became thicker as we approached

Missoula. Once past Missoula, nothing could be seen above the tree line except whiteish-grey plumes of smoke.

In the morning, we caught an early breakfast at the hotel and drove to the fly shop in Melrose. While driving eastward on the highway to Dillon, we saw an uncontrolled forest fire kicking up more smoke in the valley.

At the fly shop, we met up with our guide, Rick, a math professor at Montana Tech. We have fished with Rick since I first started fishing on the Big Hole. Rick had a big smile and the years of guiding had strengthened his legs so much that he had the calf muscles of an Olympian. He said that the water level on the Big Hole was too low. But we would not have the same problem on the Beaverhead, where the water was controlled by a dam. The Beaverhead was a narrow river with thick brush on each side that leaves only tight spaces to cast. It was also a deep river with big brown trout lying low in some holes.

On the drive to Dillon, Rick discussed the state of the Big Hole River. The fires and low water level concerned everyone – fisherman, ranchers, locals, and tourists. Hoot Owl restrictions had recently been imposed in some sections of the river and it was possible that the Montana Department of Fish & Wildlife might close the entire river in August. The ranchers were benefitting from irrigation technology that had improved to the point where the irrigation system captured all the water it removed from the river. Before the technology improved, water not captured would release back into the river. But at the time, ranchers could take out as much water as they needed, and the river suffered. In this year's drought, the ranchers were able to take even more water out of the river.

On the Beaverhead, the river was muddy and the water level was high, which was a sign that more water had recently been released from the dam, likely to help the ranchers. To make it easier for the fish to see our flies, Rick set us up with two nymphs on each of our lines and a lot of weight so that the flies would sink closer to the bottom.

Casting that heavy of a setup was tremendously difficult. With that much weight, it felt like someone had put a lead ball at the end of our lines. All we could do was heave the rod back and forward. The line would twist in the air and the flies and weight would plop into the water.

We did not have much luck in the morning. But we kept trying to make the heavy setup work. As we curled around one bend, a fish jumped up a slim channel breaking off from the river. Rick dropped the anchor and switched me to a dry fly. Water splashed around as the fish rose again about twenty yards ahead of us. Rick tried to row closer, but, after waiting awhile without any movement, we knew the fish had spooked.

After pulling the raft onto a gravel bar for a quick lunch, we embarked on the last couple hours of the trip. The river widened out more in that section, which allowed the fast current to spread and slow down. Some fishable pools developed and Rick switched my fly setup to a Chubby Chernobyl on top and a nymph on the bottom.

As we floated, Rick directed us to cast closer to the bank. We tried to mimic a fly dropping off the bank and floating right by the side. But casting too close to the bushes overhanging the river's edge risked another snag that would tear off the flies.

As I casted, the motion began to recede to the background of my mind. I only thought of where I wanted the fly to go. My limbs were sore and felt heavy and numb. All I heard was the whoosh of the fly line above me.

The right bank of the river twisted and turned in sections. Each turn sent my Chubby Chernobyl drifting farther away. As the river undulated, I placed my casts to get the best drifts. Finally, one turn led to a slight bend that created a pool of slow water. Sensing an opportunity, I cast again and hoped the fly would land where the fast and slow water merged. It did. In a moment, I saw a beautiful yellow and brown trout flash to the surface close to my fly. Its tail

whipped and body curved in the water. It then rolled over expos-
ing the white of its belly and sucked in the fly. My line immediately tightened and I held the rod tip up higher as the fish darted
away from the boat. Keeping the line tight, the fish zig-zagged and
fought until I could bring it close enough to the boat for Rick to
scoop it up in his net. After patiently waiting all day to catch something, a big brown trout on the line was like an answer to a prayer.
I felt both relieved and rejuvenated.

The purest experience in fly fishing is catching fish on a dry fly.
It requires extra concentration. But that concentration helps you
notice finer details about the water and your surroundings. When
a fish emerges and gulps down a fly, everything else around you
disappears and your mind centers on the action in front of you. It
is like watching a colorful painting develop in front of your eyes.

After catching the brown trout on the Chubby Chernobyl, we
continued down the river and I was able to redeem the day by catching a couple more browns on a dry fly.

On the drive back to the fly shop, Rick was tired and frustrated.
He looked out at the road and said that he had been guiding on the
Beaverhead for over thirty years and had never seen the river as
difficult as it was that day.

Back at the fly shop, the tall shop manager waited behind the
counter. He had a genial persona and the long hair of a traveler.
He said that he had worked in fly shops in other states and recently
worked in Northern California, but had always wanted to move to
Montana. Now, though, he wondered about the state of fly fishing
in Montana. What would fly fishing be like in thirty years on the Big
Hole River? Would it become like fishing in drier states in the west
where you only chase after trout in the beginning of the season?

As we drove away, the conversation at the fly shop left a discour-
aging impression. The ability to fish the Big Hole River during the
peak summer months of July and August had always been a reliable
part of life. Even fifteen years earlier, we could spend a day fishing

on the river during those months and catch around thirty fish each. But with an extended fire season cutting into those days, it started to seem like that reality may be slowly fading away.

As we drove back to Butte for dinner, plumes of dark smoke billowed in the sky like a smokestack. The fire would continue to burn for weeks throughout the summer. The river was more threatened than it had ever been.

EIGHTEEN

RIVER SONGS

After a couple weeks at the lake during the middle of summer, Sam, Billie Grace, Bo, and I returned to Billings. Sam kept careful watch over Billie Grace each day. Since Billie Grace would usually not wake up until later in the morning, I decided to slip away early one Saturday to fish Rock Creek once more.

When I arrived at the access site right before Red Lodge, I saw two fishermen upriver in a spot where I wanted to be. While I was putting my rod together, I saw another fisherman in waders slowly walking to another good fishing spot. I knew that the best fishing was in the early morning hours when the fish were hungry and with the creek already crowded my options were becoming severely limited by the minute.

From recent nights of intermittent sleep, I also had a pounding headache. So, as I tried to carefully pierce the tippet through the hole at the top of the grasshopper fly, I opened an app on my phone and played a song by the Grateful Dead. As I tightened the knot on the grasshopper fly, the cosmic melody of "Dark Star" filled the air and eased the drubbing pain in my head.

Sometimes it was beneficial to find a place in nature to relax and enjoy the world around me. In *Song of Myself,* Walt Whitman wrote:

"I loafe and invite my soul,

I lean and loafe at my ease observing a spear of summer grass."[11]

Fly fishing can provide that experience, even when you do not catch any fish.

Because the river was already crowded with a few other fishermen, I thought that it may turn out to be one of those days where it was best to relax and enjoy my surroundings on the river.

To get to the river, I had to manage my way down a steep cliff that led to a forest and then to the creek. By that time, I had been fishing Rock Creek for eight years. And eight years can wear on your body. When I first fished Rock Creek, I had no difficulty managing the steepness of the hill. But now I needed to grab ahold of branches on my way down to balance myself and hope that my boots did not slip on the rocks underneath.

After carefully descending the hill and walking through the forest, I saw that the creek was only a trickle of its usual self. The advantage of fishing a creek was the way the water winds downstream. It was not swift and strong like the current of a wider river. It moved in a luxurious manner, taking its time as it twisted and turned through and around rocks. But that advantage was now gone. The water was so low that grey rocks that would usually form the riverbed now lined the side of the creek. And large rocks that would otherwise serve as good hiding spots for trout now stuck out in the middle section of the creek like bare boulders.

The bottom of the river was slippery, and I was lucky that I did not fall and crack my rod into pieces. But I did find one good section where riffles dropped into a slightly deep pool. I had set up my line with a small dry fly on top and dropped a nymph about a foot below. I casted out and tracked the dry fly as it fell into the little pool. After a couple casts, I felt a slight tug on the line and saw a silver sparkle beneath the surface. A tiny rainbow had taken the nymph and it did not put up much of a fight. I reeled in the line and took the hook out as quickly as possible. As the tiny rainbow swam back to the depths of the little pool, I felt relieved. With the recent hot weather and low water levels, things were likely rough enough on the tiny fish.

After catching one fish for the day, I walked upriver for another mile, but I paid more attention to the river than the fishing. I stared into the depths of the forest and tracked the line where dry land met the water. When I stepped into the water, I felt the current push against my boot. In the distance, I saw another tiny fish rise to the surface. It danced, darted, and disappeared below. Once the little fish departed, I saw splatches of sunlight shimmering on the swaying tides of the creek. And I listened as the current spilled over ledges, slid over flat rocks, and splashed against itself. In that moment, I had forgotten about the music I listened to and how my head had ached. I was attuned to the river playing its own song.

NINETEEN

FIRE SEASON: PART II

I opened the text message and saw a picture of a ball of bright orange embers burning on the mountainside across Skidoo Bay. A video showed a plane descending into the bay to scoop up water to douse the fire. My family took those pictures and videos while looking out at the fire spreading on the mountain across the water on Flathead Lake.

At night, sections of red burning light on the Mission Mountains glowed in the middle of darkness and was not far from rows of houses on the shoreline. It was like destruction peered over the shoulders of the helpless homes. Evenings were usually cool at the lake, but it stayed warm that night. Strong winds breathed more life into the fire and it burst from around 150 acres to over 1,000 acres.

After midnight, the fire department called my parents landline and told them to be ready to evacuate. If the winds kept up, the fire could shift onto Finley Point. My family members each packed a bag of clothes and rushed out the door before the mandatory evacuation took effect.

A gym in Polson served as the center for the displaced residents of the point. My family hunkered down at a friend's cabin near Bigfork for a couple days not knowing when they could return. As they waited, they nervously read updates on the fire online. At least they were all safe.

I could keep up with the fire by reading updates on social media. Some residents provided their home address and confirmed that they did evacuate. Some residents asked the fire department for recommendations on what they should do with their horses or cattle. A rescue group from Ronan, about 15 miles from Polson, said they could pick up any abandoned horses in their horse trailer and bring them to their ranch. The fire department told the cattle owners to put their cellphone numbers on the cattle and someone would return the cattle once the evacuation order lifted. People posted pictures of a cat stranded on a rocky cliff being rescued and a dog standing all alone on a dock being saved by some Good Samaritans.

That night, the fire jumped over the highway and burned some of the homes and other buildings on the eastside of Skidoo Bay. Highway 35, which runs up the eastside of the lake, was shut down and would be for the foreseeable future.

A few summers back, a forest fire burned near Woods Bay, which was further up Finley Point. The fire near Woods Bay started close to the lake, but proceeded to spread up and over the mountains into the Swan Valley. It was likely that the Boulder 2700 would do the same. But that was no solace for the people who already lost their homes.

During that week, I decided to keep my fishing ritual going and try my luck on the Bighorn River over the weekend. I stopped at the fly shop in Billings on Friday and picked up some more hoppers and nymphs. I asked whether a worm might work and the guide recommended a long red worm with a tungsten steel ball in the middle. He said the tungsten steel would help make the worm drop to the bottom.

On my early morning drive to the Bighorn, I saw that the fires outside of Hardin had not subdued. After I took the exit for Route 90 out of Billings, the normally wide-open sky was covered with white smoke. The fire had expanded to 65,000 acres and smoke blanketed everything in sight. The sun, too, was a blood red color like the core of a grapefruit. It reminded me of the ominous sun portrayed in old Western movies where the hero was stuck in the desert heat running out of time and water.

In the dim light of the early morning, I stopped at a gas station in Hardin and the smoke was so close that it came through the air vents. A fire crew from Phoenix pulled up to the gas pump across from me. The men in the truck all looked like they had not slept for days. Their hair was disheveled and their clothes were caked in greyish soot.

Bad omens appeared on the way to the river. Out of nowhere, a black crow swooped in from the side and hit my front fender with a thud. I saw a lost dog meandering by the side of the road. It bent its neck up to see what was coming. I flashed my lights at the truck approaching in the oncoming lane and hoped that the dog would not step into the road.

Once at the river, I again tried my luck at the Three Mile access site. As I walked down the dirt path leading from the parking lot, I saw that the water in the usual spots that I fished was low and tepid. In the crystal clearness of the water, I could tell that no fish were around. I casted out a few times, but got no bites.

With no luck at Three Mile, I decided to check out either After-bay, where the dam was located, or the Bighorn access site located about seven miles farther up the road, where the water could get murky. At Afterbay, there was a traffic jam of trucks ready to slide drift boats into the river at the put-in spot. I walked along the bank, but the water was too low and no clear place to wade out could be found. So I drove back up the road along the river to the Bighorn access site.

At the Bighorn access site, the water was deeper and warmer than at Three Mile. But the water near the put-in spot was also tinged with sandy sediment from the riverbed. I decided to see if I could find a better spot downriver. With my rod in hand, I walked past lodges and homes until I found a spot where the water looked like it might hold some fish.

After a few casts, I felt a slight tug and saw a small rainbow trout emerge from the deep. It was not much bigger than the one I caught earlier in the season on Rock Creek. I eased the hook out of its mouth and let the little rainbow swim back to freedom.

As I let the little rainbow go, I wondered if all I would have to show for my adventures over the past few weeks would be a total of two small trout.

After catching the rainbow trout on the Bighorn, I continued down the bank and saw in the distance that a rusty old farm tractor jutted out from the bank into the river. I would not be able to proceed past that point. But, before that point, a spring creek flowed through the adjacent ranch and poured into the river. In the depths of where the creek and river met, a school of brown trout moved and shifted. I perched my head around the tall bushes to see if I could cast upward into the creek, and I saw slightly enough room to cast. Nearby, I also observed small tan-winged insects jumping all over the rocks and into the grass on the bank.

For the next hour, I casted into the creek and threw the kitchen sink at the school of trout. I used every fly bought at the fly shop in Fort Smith to see if anything would catch their attention. I rigged up various patterns of caddis nymphs, PMDs, sowbugs, and hoppers. After a while, I lost track of which fly was which. Some flies were fluffy and tan, some were black with yellow or red streaks, and others were grey with splatches of orange.

I am glad that I did not give up. In an instant, I felt a huge pull on the line. All the nearby trout scattered and I could feel this fish dive down deep into the river. I also knew that this fish could be a big one – maybe even a three pounder. That was the kind of fish I had been longing to catch on the Bighorn each time I went out that summer. As the line tightened, I bent farther back and felt a jolt in my bicep muscles from the force of the pulling fish. The fish kept tugging away from me and I kept fighting to bring it closer. Suddenly I felt a snap and my line went limp. The giant monster pulled so hard that it broke off my line. It was supposed to be my redemption, but now that was gone.

After that tough loss, I had enough of fishing the murky little creek. A few yards up, I saw other trout in a holding pattern at the bottom of the river. Most likely, they were trying to rest. As I moved closer, I kept an eye on them and casted above where they were stationed. Some of the browns were so big that their fins protruded out from the top of the water.

As the day progressed, the temperature rose and the sun beat down on me. I started to feel the sweat on my forehead drip down my face. But I kept fishing.

I casted over the heads of the big monsters in the deep and prayed that one of them would take a bite of one of the nymphs I had on the line. Unfortunately, they were either not hungry, or picky eaters. Like a puppeteer, I made the nymphs on my line dance below the water surface in hopes of catching the attention of one of the browns. Watching the flies bounce by the lazing trout seemed like a cruel joke each time it happened.

One giant brown trout suddenly had enough of the charade. It powered through the water like a shark. The giant brown trout took a big gulp and swallowed the fly. I kept the rod tip high and the line as tight as I could, but the brown was an immovable object. In some imperceptible language, it signaled that I was not going to catch it. It rose out of the water with force and spit the fly at the end of my line back at me. I was pulling so hard on the line when the fly came loose that it darted way behind me and got caught in the tall grass. I also lost my balance and stumbled a few steps backwards. The heart-pounding exhilaration of landing one of the biggest fish of my life yielded to bitter disappointment. Once again, I had been bested.

After another loss, I wiped the sweat out of my eyes with my muddied shirt. Each time further blinding myself. With salt burning in my eyes and wildfire smoke surrounding me, I decided that I had finally reached the end of my pain tolerance for the day.

Sometimes fly fishing teaches you that the only wisdom to be gained is the wisdom of humility.

TWENTY

THE BRINK OF COLLAPSE

I thought about trying to fish the Bighorn again the next weekend, but the Richland Springs fire, not far away on the Northern Cheyenne Reservation, continued to burn and had expanded to an area of 170,000 acres in eastern Montana. Mandatory evacuations for residents in towns on the reservation were a possibility. The fire had also jumped across the highway that runs through the reservation. I decided that another day of fishing was not worth the risk.

On the other side of the state, the wildfire near Wise River in the Big Hole Valley continued to burn into August. An article in the *Montana Standard* stated that the fire was one of the longest forest fires ever in the valley.[12] The uncertainty from the fire had taken a severe toll on the people who lived nearby. A store clerk confessed that the fire caused him depression that felt like a weight. A firefighter said that the fire season had physically killed the bodies of the firefighters. The article also warned that long-term health effects from breathing in smoke may include an increased risk of cardiovascular disease. Finally, one local noted that it was the river that was "in the saddest shape of all."

The plight of the rivers in Montana during drought and fire season caught the attention of national media. A headline in the *New York Times* read: "Montana's Famed Trout Under Threat as Drought Intensifies."[13] The articled noted that the severe drought and other extreme weather conditions may not be a temporary problem and the state's fisheries could be "nearing collapse." The collapse of the river systems would also tank the state's outdoor economy.

The effects on fish population were tragic. The article referenced dead fish floating in some rivers. A recent study found a steep decline in fish populations. On the Big Hole River, the number of brown trout per mile decreased from around 1,800 per mile only a few years ago in 2014, to around a meager 400 per mile in May 2021.

The fish that survived were subject to higher water temperatures. Trout need water temperatures in the range of 45 to 60 degrees to thrive. Water temperatures around 75 degrees can be lethal to these fish. The article noted that temperatures in some rivers hit the low 70s much earlier than usual this summer. At that level, the fish become lethargic because of less oxygen in the water and they quit feeding. Worse, the stress of being caught by fishermen in that weakened state can kill them.

Echoing what we learned about the Big Hole River earlier in the summer, the article indicated that ranchers used to primarily flood irrigate their fields, which returned about half the water to the river system. But now many use pivot irrigation systems, which are far more efficient and use nearly all the water.

The decline in trout populations was believed to be caused by the "shifting river conditions caused by climate change." Worried for the future, a guide on the Missouri River concluded that the extreme changes were "… starting to feel like a downward spiral."

TWENTY-ONE

BATTLE ON THE BIGHORN

By late August, the Richland Fire had been contained and the smoke in the sky started to clear up. With cleaner air to breathe, I decided to try one more Saturday on the Bighorn River.

At the fly shop in Fort Smith, rows of trucks and drift boats lined the perimeter of the parking lot. Two hunting dogs, a black one with an orange tennis ball in its mouth and a white one with black spots, darted in and out of the fly shop with their tails wagging. I picked up some caddis and PMD flies inside the shop and headed to the Afterbay access site.

At Afterbay, a forty-foot-high concrete dam intersects the river. At the top of the dam is a bridge that runs over the river. Water rushes out into the river through spaces in the dam's wall. Running across the river about thirty yards up from the dam is a cable. A sign on the river's edge says that no boating or wading is allowed past the cable. I assumed that the undercurrent must be strong enough that someone swimming in that section would get sucked into the dam.

I had gotten a late start that day and fishermen were already putting their drift boats into the water at the access site. I walked about four yards up from the put-in ramp and waded out into the water. Close to the rocky bank, the water was shallow and calm. But out in the middle, it was a little faster and choppy.

I waded out as far as I could before the riverbed precipitously dropped. The water closer to me was a bright shade of green, but it changed to a deep blue farther out. I casted out into the deep blue and watched as my orange indicator drifted by in the fast current.

After a few casts, I moved closer to the deep water near the dam and casted directly at the cable wire. I stripped and mended my line to keep it moving in the choppy water, but it felt like I had already missed my opportunity for the day.

After one long cast, the orange bobber dipped and my chest pounded. I saw the orange bobber thrash and suddenly the bright, silver belly of a rainbow trout rolled around in the water. I immediately set the hook as my line shot in different, jagged directions in front of me. It had been a while since I had a good-sized fish on the line. I let the rainbow run before I brought it back in. The reel made a zipping sound as I let more and more line out. I pointed the rod tip high in the sky and firmly started to reel the line back in. After fighting a little more, I was able to bring the fish in close enough to see the pinkish-red splotch of red splashed on its silvery side. I took one moment to admire the rainbow trout, unhooked it, and let it wiggle back to the depths of the river.

I felt a wave a relief roll through me. Some tension had been built up. I had, probably unnecessarily, placed stress on myself to catch a good-sized trout. But kneeling to take the hook out of the rainbow, I again felt that kinetic connection to the world around me.

Before leaving Fort Smith, I took a quick drive up the road to the Bighorn Canyon, which was one of the marvels of Montana. The road up twisted and turned over hills and through fields of yellow and green brush. At the end of the road was a lake with a little marina and a few docks for boats.

At the marina, I looked out at the red rocky cliffs ascending out of the deep blue water of the lake. The red on the rocks reminded me of the brush of red on the side of the rainbow trout I had caught. A breeze drifted through and the sunlight on the lake water shimmered by the cliffs.

Before leaving the canyon, I imagined the dark sky at night and the contrast of the shades of red at sunset. Beyond the dam, the canyon continued and the river carved out a deeper space. Nature provided many spectacular settings, but perhaps none as sublime as a river that curves through a red rock canyon into a vast land beyond.

TWENTYTWO

CHANNELING HEMINGWAY
AT PILOT CREEK

In October, I planned a mini-vacation for our family and rented a cabin in Cooke City, Montana for the weekend. Cooke City is an old-mining town perched at 7,800 feet elevation in the Yellowstone High Country on the outskirts of Yellowstone National Park. Only around 100 people live in Cooke City throughout the year and it receives an average of 200 inches of snow annually.[14]

As we drove from Billings through Paradise Valley, we stopped at Sage Lodge near Pray for lunch. We strolled through the doors of the lodge and into the grand lobby with towering windows that overlooked a pond stocked with trout in the foreground and a snow-capped mountain in the background. After leaving Sage Lodge, we followed the highway down to Gardiner, Montana.

In Gardiner, I visited the local fly shop to see if I could pick up some recommendations for spots to fish in or near Yellowstone and flies to use. The shop was in an old, historic building. The owner said that he had been running the fly shop since the 1970s when his father passed away. He suggested grasshopper and Copper John flies for either Soda Butte Creek inside the park or the Clark's Fork River outside of it. I bought a few of each.

After passing by the Roosevelt Arch at the north entrance to the park, we drove into Mammoth Hot Springs. Although it was in the park, Mammoth Hot Springs was like a small town with a courthouse, post office, and grand hotel. If we continued south, we could have walked up the boardwalks to explore the geothermal hot springs where scalding water rose through limestone rocks. Instead, we took a left at Mammoth and drove through Lamar Valley. Shoulder season – late spring or early fall – is one of the best times to drive through the park. The crowds have thinned, the weather is mild and plenty of wildlife can be seen. The leaves on the trees along the road had already started to turn bright yellow and orange. Herds of buffalo wandered in the fields in the distance. It was like stepping into a scene from one of Albert Bierstadt's paintings of buffalo in Yellowstone in the mid-19th century. I spotted one fly fisherman trapesing though Soda Butte Creek, but the water looked too shallow to fish.

In Cooke City, we first stopped at the Cooke City General Store at the beginning of town. The general store was located inside a big two-story building painted the same color of red as a firetruck. It had all types of regular grocery supplies. The front corner of the store also had a little fly shop – or, more appropriately, a fly fishing stand. The store was owned by a married couple who likely managed it during tourist season and closed it up in late September. Unfortunately, the husband who ran the fly fishing stand was not in the store at the time.

After the general store, we checked into the small log cabin we rented on Main Street. The cabin did not have a television, but it did have internet access. Out the back door, I walked onto a wooden porch that overlooked the mountain range. Below the mountains, a small creek trickled over rocks. Next door to the cabin was a two-story building with rows of snowmobiles lined up on the first-floor porch. Up in the high altitude of the Beartooth Mountains, the roads could be impassable during some points in the offseason. Those snowmobiles were likely the best way to get around.

Samantha, Billie Grace, Bo, and I settled in at the cabin and picked out one of the few open restaurants, which served Malaysian food, to order takeout from. After picking up dinner, I stopped into a convenience shop attached to a motor lodge. In the shop, I noticed a book that I had read earlier in the year called *Ernest Hemingway in the Yellowstone High Country* by Chris Warren. The book had prompted my fascination with Cooke City and was the reason why we went on the trip.

Ernest Hemingway was born in 1899 in the Oak Park, Illinois, a suburban village outside of Chicago. At 18, he joined the Italian Front during World War I and was seriously wounded by mortar fire. In 1923, he moved to Paris and joined the Lost Generation of writers that included James Joyce, Ezra Pound, and Gertrude Stein. A couple years later, he published his first successful novel, *The Sun Also Rises*.

Hemingway wrote about fishing adventures on the Irati River in Spain in *The Sun Also Rises*, and also about the Upper Peninsula in Michigan in the two semi-autobiographical short stories *Big Two-Hearted River*. But he did not truly become a fly fisherman until he spent summers in the Yellowstone High Country in the 1930s.

Hemingway lived with his wife, Pauline, and three sons at a ranch in Wyoming near Cooke City for five summers in between 1930 and 1939. He only took a break in between 1936 and 1938 to cover the Loyalist cause in the Spanish Civil War.[15]

In the Yellowstone High Country, Hemingway and his family experienced a lifetime of adventure. In the backcountry, he hunted for elk, bighorn sheep, and bears. With his wife, they fished the Clark's

Fork River and backcountry lakes. The family became friends with the local guides and ranchers, and he taught his boys how to ride horseback. He was the first person to drive over the Clark's Fork River in a car.[16] He found a good drinking spot called Hoosiers Bar across from the general store. And, although his personal life is usually portrayed as volatile, he was a good husband and a good father to his sons during those summers in Montana.

The vacations also influenced his writing. In one of the first summers, Hemingway broke his arm in a car accident with the novelist and friend, John Dos Passos, outside of Billings and spent six weeks at Saint Vincent's Hospital.[17] His stay at the hospital in Billings was the genesis for the short story, *The Gambler, The Nun, and the Radio.*

Hemingway also said that Cooke City was one of the best places for him to write along with Paris, Madrid and Key West.[18] He worked on *Death in the Afternoon, To Have and Have Not,* and many short stories during his time in the Yellowstone High Country.[19] He mailed many of those works, including a final manuscript for *Death in the Afternoon,* off at the Cooke City General Store.[20] The general store was also mentioned in the fictional memoir, *True at First Light.*[21] Some of the scenes in the mountains of Spain in the novel *For Whom the Bell Tolls* were inspired by his trips into the backcountry near Cooke City. Not surprisingly, the main character in *For Whom the Bell Tolls,* Robert Jordan, was originally from nearby Red Lodge, Montana.[22]

Hemingway also confronted the painful memory of his father's suicide during those trips. In one scene from *For Whom the Bell Tolls,* Robert Jordan recalled a time when he rode horses in the backcountry of the Beartooth Mountains with his friend, Chub Weaver. Jordan dismounted from his horse and threw the Smith and Wesson revolver that his father used to kill himself into the bottom of a lake. Chub Weaver confirmed that event happened in real life. Weaver remembered that, on one trip into the Beartooths, Hemingway took the revolver that his father had used to commit suicide and threw in into the bottom of Froze-to-Death Lake on the Beartooth Plateau.[23]

In the morning, I stepped back into the Cooke City General Store because I needed a Wyoming fishing license. In Wyoming, you can only fish on public lands; otherwise, you are trespassing on private property. The owner who ran the fly stand was fortunately back at the store. I looked at the selection and asked for some fly recommendations. He recommended Royal Coachman and black caddis flies. He also suggested fishing anywhere on a 10-to-15-mile section of the river along the Chief Joseph Highway in Wyoming. He said to try to fish for about an hour at a spot, and, if that does not work out, then find another spot.

Before I left, I noticed the same Hemingway book at the general store and I asked the owner about it. He stood behind a sparkling gold cash register and said that it was the same register used in the 1930s when Hemingway would frequent the general store. I stood in amazement and took in what it may have been like to see Hemingway walk in to deliver a manuscript. Before I left, I thanked the owner for the advice about the Clark's Fork. He nodded back and declared that Hemingway used to "fish the hell out of the Clark's Fork."

I jumped back into my truck and headed down to the Chief Joseph Scenic Highway. Along the road, I saw a cowboy wearing a long black jacket on top of a horse. Ahead of him were a few black cattle. I gathered that cattle were allowed to roam freely outside of Cooke City.

It was difficult to find a good place along the highway to access the Clark's Fork. I passed by Pilot Creek and drove farther down the road. Along the way, I saw a sign for the Nordquist Ranch. Hemingway had stayed at the L-Bar Ranch during his summers in the Beartooths and the L-Bar was owned by the Nordquist family. But the Nordquist's divorced not long after Hemingway left and it was possible that the husband started his own ranch.

I drove up and down the highway without finding an obvious place to fish. Wyoming was not like Montana where the fishing access sites were clearly marked. On the drive back up, I pulled over at a scenic pull-off on the highway. A rocky hill led straight down to the river. I could see big boulders in the river and white water gushing though narrow sections between them. But farther down, the river opened and I thought that the calmer water might be a decent spot to fish. I tied the Royal Coachman fly onto the line and walked down to the river.

By the river I saw a variety of different tracks, none of which looked like bear tracks. Along the bank were a few piles of fresh dung that, I thought or at least hoped, were from cattle. I did have a can of bear spray looped around my belt, but I was so tired from lack of good sleep at that point that a bear could have tapped me on the shoulder without me noticing.

Out of curiosity, I first walked upriver and climbed over some of the big boulders to see if I could find any good fishing spots. I saw some deep pools between where the cold water rushed through openings between the grey boulders. I casted a few times into the pools without any success. I next tried a few casts in the shallow section, hoping not to catch a glimpse of a bear out of the corner of my eye. After a half-hour, I took the general store owner's advice and decided to find a new spot.

I drove back up the Chief Joseph Scenic Highway and pulled into a campground site on Pilot Creek. When I stepped out of the truck, I could hear the soft gurgling of the creek not far away. I followed it down to where it connected with the Clark's Fork. The Clark's Fork at that section abutted next to the highway. Below the bridge over the highway, I spotted a lone fisherman casting out to where the creek and river merged.

Something drew me to that spot of the river. It was peaceful and untouched. I later learned that the section where Pilot Creek and the Clark's Fork meet was Hemingway's favorite spot to fish. He may have had a spiritual connection to the same place I was now about to fish.

I crossed over the highway hoping not to get hit by a car. Once

across, I worked my way up through the forest to put enough distance between myself and the other fisherman.

When I brushed away the branches, I saw a beautiful stretch of
river. The water was low but looked fishable. Some bends in the
river created riffles and deep holes where trout might be basking
on the river bottom. The cook at the Malaysian restaurant had recommended this spot and said that he had caught some good-sized
rainbows. Maybe he did earlier in the year, but this section was only
six inches deep in some spots – too low for a big rainbow.

I started casting out into one spot where water cascaded over a
few rocks. I looked around too. It was a beautiful fall day. The leaves
on the trees and bushes had turned yellow and orange. All the rocks
on the bottom of the river were different shades of grey, like nature's own shale walkway.

Pilot Peek was an exceptionally tall mountain with a sharp point
on the pinnacle. It was also perfectly centered in between the tips
of the evergreen lodgepole pines on each side of the river. It looked
like Ansel Adams' photo of *Half Dome and Merced River, 1935*, except that the peak on Pilot Peak looked sharp enough to cut a dia-
mond. The symmetry of the scene reminded me of looking up at
the altar and cross in an old cathedral.

I continued walking up the river, casting into spots where a little
fish might hide. A fallen tree branch created a little pool of water
in one bend of the river. The Royal Coachman fly bounced on the
water surface past the branch and into the open pool. I suddenly
felt a spark like a sharp bolt of lightning. A trout gulped down the
Royal Coachman and I tugged at the rod to set the hook. The fish
was active, but small enough that it was easy to pull in. Once it was
close enough, I reached down and lifted up a wild brook trout. I
had not caught a brook trout in years. This one looked more colorful than any brook trout that Winslow Homer painted from his
times fishing in the Adirondacks. It had a green body with vivid
black and orange spots covering its center.

After letting the first brook trout go, I continued walking upriver like an explorer who had found his bearings. My surroundings were new and, at first, I felt a little nervous about whether I would catch another fish or leave empty-handed. But after catching the first fish, I could feel my uneasiness dissipate. I felt balanced. Something told me to keep going.

Upstream, I found a slight bend where water flowed into a little pool. I fished the foam line and caught more brook trout with the same bright spots. I held each one in the water for a moment so that they could regain their strength before swimming off. Many fish also rose to look at the Royal Coachman fly, but they may have been too small to eat it.

After a couple hours of fishing the shallow section of river, I walked up to a sharp bend that was lined with more big boulders on the western edge. A mother and daughter walked on a dirt path above and carefully watched as I cast into a spot where some water descended over a small rock cliff. I bent into each cast and kept my rod tip high as I softly mended the line. The mother asked me what fly I was using and I told her about the Coachman. It had been a productive day so far, I said. She nodded in agreement and said that she had fished yesterday and did not catch anything until she used a Coachman. After she said that, my line tensed once again and another brook trout was flipping and splashing around on the end of it. I brought the trout closer in and bent down to take the hook out. I looked around and saw that I had a small audience. The mother and daughter peered down from above the rocks. The fisherman I had seen when I first got to the river was standing across the river in a parking lot with his fishing companion. They watched as I let the brook trout go. The trout was not big, but the dance of landing the fish had focused everyone's attention. It felt like nature had decided to put on a play and I was one of the actors.

After catching a few trout, I decided to call it a day. The picturesque image of Pilot Peak will stay with me. I also will not forget those colorful spots on the brook trout. And I will never forget that I fished at Ernest Hemingway favorite spot on the Clark's Fork.

In February 1939, Hemingway captured his experiences in the Yellowstone High Country in an article in *Vogue* magazine entitled "The Clark's Fork Valley, Wyoming." He wrote about how he would find the big trout in the center of the stream at the end of summer and how the native fish were "sleek, shining, and heavy" and they "leaped when they took the fly." He reminisced about "all the hunting and all the fishing and the riding in the summer sun." And he remembered his children learning to ride horseback and "how they loved the country." Finally, to end the article, he simply said: "It's a good country."[24]

If Hemingway loved that river, is it possible that his presence remained there?

TWENTYTHREE

THE CONSOLATION OF NATURE

In early October, Sam and Billie Grace traveled back to New Jersey for a short trip. I would join them in a few days, but for one weekend, I was on my own. The only thought I had was to try my luck on the Clark's Fork River again. It would be my last fly fishing trip for the year. I checked the updates on the weather in Cooke City. An early snow storm could be possible in the mountains. But it looked to be in the 50s the whole weekend. So I booked a cabin in Cooke City.

After work on Friday, I loaded up the truck with my fishing gear and Bo hopped in the back for the start of another journey. I stopped in Red Lodge for dinner at an authentic Mexican restaurant in town. Once I got back into the truck it was already dark out. I drove past Bearcreek and Belfry and crossed over the Montana-Wyoming border. I hardly saw another car along the way.

While driving the Chief Joseph Scenic Highway, I could only see yellow signs marking the side of the road as I turned each corner. Signs abruptly said to slow down to 20 miles per hour before hair-pin turns. I drove in fits and starts. If my brakes failed, Bo and I would be sent flying over the guardrails into the deep abyss below.

To my luck, the owner was in the lobby when I arrived. She said that she usually goes to bed at 9:30 pm and leaves the key in the rental cabin if the guest arrives late. But my cabin was down a dimly lit road and I would not have found it without her help. Plus, she had forgotten that I had made a reservation for that night anyway.

As I walked out of the lobby, I caught a glimpse of a man sitting in a rocking chair and talking on his phone. He excitedly told the other person on the line that he had caught a twenty-inch rainbow that day. I imagined that he had taken a guided trip to one of the backcountry lakes because the water on the nearby rivers was too low to catch anything that size.

The owner grabbed the key and started walking down a dirt road in the pitch-black darkness. I followed behind her with the head-lights of my truck illuminating her back.

The cabin harkened back to a time before electricity, television, or the internet. But it was perfect for a weekend of fly fishing.

As I approached the cabin, I had to duck to get in the front door. I noticed that the glass pane window on the door had duct-tape on the edge that kept it in place. I scanned the main room to see what my accommodations would be. A kitchen in the back corner of the room had a stovetop, oven, and a fridge. A couch with scratchy fabric was pressed against the side of the wall in the living room and a television was positioned next to it.

In the bedroom, a painting of a thirteen-point buck was centered over the middle of the king-sized bed. The windows on the walls in the bedroom used folded-paper as window curtains.

After settling in, I let Bo outside before going to bed. I looked up and saw thick and heavy stars in the night sky. The swirling galaxy of stars looked like a river winding through a deep canyon. I wondered if Hemingway had also once marveled at those same stars.

I slipped into bed and flipped through a few pages of *A Sun Also Rises* before my eyelids became heavy. I read about the nightlife in Paris where Jake and his friends bounced from one café to the next, but I slowly began to lose focus. I placed the book on the bed stand, turned off the soft glow of the bedside lamp, and sank into a deep sleep.

Early in the morning, I quickly cooked a breakfast of bacon and eggs. Bo sidled beside me and gobbled up the leftover bacon strips.

I had time to kill before the temperature warmed up on the river and ventured into town. But almost everything downtown was closed for the season.

Back at the cabin, I wandered outside to see if I could pick up an internet signal so that I could purchase a Wyoming fishing license online. A large dog sat bemusedly on the porch. A chain connected her to one of the pillars, but it was long enough for her to roam around.

The owner saw that I looked lost and came outside to help. She pointed to the blinking light in the window near the side corner of the building and said that I had to stand a few feet near it to pick up a signal. I held the phone up to the corner of the building. The sound of the dog chain clinked as the dog wandered over to see what was going on. A couple bars on the cell phone started blinking. While I was typing in my request for a license, a black falcon with a yellow collar around its neck swooped down and perched itself on a woodpile directly in front of me. I thought of the line about the falcon and falconer in W.B. Yeats' *The Second Coming*. Another falcon, this one with a blue collar, swooped in and perched next to the one with a yellow collar. They both sat on the woodpile and stared at me. My license request thankfully went through and I gingerly stepped away from the falcons.

After getting the license, I packed up the truck with my rod and fishing gear. Bo jumped into the back seat and we headed back down to the Clark's Fork River.

At the river, I parked in the same spot along Pilot Creek as before. I retraced my steps and stepped over a few boulders underneath the bridge and found a little pool of water right where the Clark's Fork met the little creek. I saw brook trout in a holding pattern and tried to see if the bright orange fly on the end of my line might turn their heads. But they were more interested in relaxing than eating.

I walked farther upriver and managed to catch one brook trout with the same colorful bright spots as I had caught before. I also glimpsed back up at the surreal Pilot Peak in the distance. But the water level was even lower than before and I did not expect to catch many fish. So I packed the truck back up and decided to try the Clark's Fork Trailhead.

While I drove up the highway lined with lodgepole pine, I glanced at the black cows wandering along the side of the road. Somewhere not far behind were probably two old cowboys like Gus McCrae and Woodrow Call, the two cowboys and best friends from Larry McMurtry's epic Western novel, *Lonesome Dove*.

At the trailhead, a wooden walkway led down to the river. At the river's edge, I saw fishermen standing below a huge boulder and casting out into a pool of water. I walked farther upriver through some thick brush and found a rocky area where the river narrowed into a stream. I fished the seams on the sides of rocks in the middle of the stream. But the water was also low and barely flowed over the rocky bottom of the river. So I trekked back through the thick brush and headed to the cabin for a quick lunch.

I almost quit fishing that day. By mid-afternoon, the air had cooled and the fish were most likely too lethargic. But I had never fished in Yellowstone Park, so I decided to head west and take my chances.

While driving past the northeast entrance to the park, I peered down at Soda Butte Creek as it winded through the steep walls of Ice Box Canyon. I imagined fishing in the darkness of the deep canyon. Past the canyon and down at lower elevation, I entered the Lamar Valley. Tourists on the side of the road pressed binoculars against their eyes to see bison lazing in the distance.

I kept driving until I arrived at the Lamar River. But the water was also too low. I doubled back to Soda Butte Creek and pulled into a parking lot by the creek without any other cars in sight.

The remaining light of the day was already starting to fade and every ten minutes meant slightly less natural light. After setting up my rod, I walked past some picnic tables and stepped down the rocky bank to the creek.

After a few unsuccessful casts, I found the only deep pool in that stretch of the creek. I casted to where the riffles rushed over an edge of rocks into the slow pool. The fly dipped and bobbed over a little waterfall and gently floated into the serene water. Like a bolt of lightning, a black-spotted trout suddenly gulped the fly and chased off towards branches near the bank. While the trout tried to tangle the line, I wiggled my boots to get better footing in the rocks and raised my rod high in the air. The rod waved side-to-side like a scepter during a ceremony. I tried to get the trout back into the pool so that it would swim around and tire it out. But it kept fighting. After another minute, the shock wore off for the trout and it lost its might. I was able to draw it closer and dipped my hands in the water before picking it up. After I took the hook out, the trout darted back into the depths of Soda Butte Creek.

Afterwards, I gazed down the lonely river. The day had been a disappointment until that point. But, while the last light lingered, I was able to catch my first fish in Yellowstone National Park. I looked upriver again and the darkness prevented me from pressing any farther.

At night, I headed over to the Miner's Saloon in Cooke City for pizza. A big red-and-blue Grateful Dead sign hung on the front side of the restaurant. Stepping inside, I heard the guitar chords and lyrics from "St. Stephen" ripping through the air.

I found the last seat at the bar and ordered a bourbon and coke on the rocks. The bartender saw my sweatshirt that I bought in Whitefish with the name of the town on it and gave me an approving nod. He fist-bumped another patron at the bar while they both said, "Go Griz!" The Griz were the University of Montana's football team and they were playing on the television screen against Eastern Washington University on an orange-colored football field.

As I took my fist sip of bourbon, the jukebox switched to the next Grateful Dead song. I soon caught on that the playlist consisted of mostly Grateful Dead songs. A light mood swept through the restaurant as "Morning Dew" played. Around the restaurant, people laughed and bit off slices of pizza and told stories to each other.

When the bartended took my order, I asked him when the restaurant became a Grateful Dead bar. He said that it had been that way for the last twelve years. But it was up for sale and who knew if they would continue to keep it as a Grateful Dead bar.

When the bartender stepped away, I heard him talk about the history of the place to a couple other patrons seated at the bar. The building was originally built in 1932 as a garage, but it probably did not become a restaurant until the 1970s. I remembered from the book that 1932 was one of the summers that Hemingway vacationed with his family in Cooke City. He may have stopped at that same location when it was a garage.

I saw that the same Hemingway book I had read was propped up against a few liquor bottles behind the bar. When the bartender wandered back over, I pointed and mentioned that it was a good book. "Yeah, you liked it?" the bartender responded. I nodded with affirmation. He then said, "Thanks, I wrote it!" I had pictured the author to be someone in a cardigan who typed out his book on his laptop at the local café. Instead, the friendly bartender was the true author.

He said that he lived in Cooke City year-round and he kept hearing stories about the summers that Hemingway spent in the Yellowstone High Country in the 1930s. The son of Chub Weaver, one of

Hemingway's best friends, continued to live on a ranch nearby in Wyoming. So, he started interviewing some of the old-timers and it turned into a book. He was fortunate to be able preserve those stories. Otherwise, they would have been lost for all eternity.

Before settling my tab, the bartended asked me what I was doing up in Cooke City. I said I tried fishing on the Clark's Fork but the water was too low. He nodded at a couple guys sitting at the end of the bar. They were fishing guides, and they also told him that fishing was rough that day.

I mentioned that I might try to fish Trout Lake in the park in the morning. It seemed aptly named, at least. The bartender grinned and said that to catch fish on Trout Lake you need a boat that will get out into the middle of the lake. That is where you might find some fish.

The next morning, I took my chances at Trout Lake anyway. Before walking up the trailhead, I unintentionally scared a couple tourists when I mentioned that I hoped we would not encounter any grizzly bears on the trail. I then awkwardly left the conversation and started on the dirt path. On the way up to the lake, I looked over the crest of a hill and could see acres of rolling pines in an untouched forest.

At the lake, I stretched out my arm muscles and tried to cast the line as far out toward the middle of the lake as I could. But I should have listened to the bartender. The fly drifted peacefully in the water after each cast. I did not have any strikes that day.

After an hour, I reeled in my line one last time for the year and headed back down the trail. Although I only caught one fish that trip, it was not a loss. On the way down, I looked up at the blue October sky covering the snowy mountains in Yellowstone Park like a blanket. I took in a one last deep breath of crisp fall air. My ritual of fly fishing during the year was now complete. Maybe in time I could gather what I had learned. But, in that moment, I left knowing that being in nature was a worthwhile consolation.

TWENTY-FOUR

CHASING THE BIG FISH

Chasing after something greater than yourself is one of the themes of Norman Maclean's fly fishing story in *A River Runs Through It*. Maclean's brother, Paul, had a talent for finding the big trout in the river. Paul invented the novel technique of shadow casting as a way of luring those big trout to the top of the water. And Paul had the strength and supernatural ability to wade into the depths of the river, almost being swept away by it, in pursuit of the biggest fish.

The pursuit of the big fish also captures the religious nature of the sport. A fisherman experiences no greater agony than losing the big fish and no greater ecstasy than landing the big one.

Throughout my year of delving further into the experience of fly fishing, I learned a lot about myself and about fishing. But, during that time, I had not landed a single big fish. In the summer of 2022, I knew that had to change.

In October 2021, I zipped up my fly rod in its case and packed it away in my bedroom closet. Next to it I placed my green duffel bag full of reels, fishing vest, and an assortment of flies. I dropped my fishing boots in the garage not knowing whether they would make it through the freezing cold winter. I put all that gear away and waited for spring to arrive.

We had a generally mild winter in Montana in 2021, but, at least near Billings, we got a lot of precipitation in the spring. It rained a lot in Billings, but, in the distance, you could see the snow piling up on the mountain peaks.

In mid-May, we celebrated my daughter's first birthday. We turned her birthday celebration into an adventure of our own. We had birthday cake in Billings and drove to the Sage Lodge near Pray for a birthday lunch. At night, we stayed in a hotel aside the Yellowstone River in Gardiner.

Tourist season had not yet begun and the line to get into Yellowstone National Park the next morning was short. We took the winding road from Gardiner down to Mammoth Hot Springs. The road hedges so close to the mountain cliff that in some spots all that exists between the mountain and the river is the road.

In Mammoth Hot Springs, we visited the historic hotel and nearby general store. We drove up to some of the hot springs and got out of the car to look at the steam emanating from the cauldron of hot pools.

Afterwards, we headed east through Lamar Valley to get to Cooke City. Along the way, we saw a stampede of buffalo thundering through the valley. Their thick, dark hair flowed through the air and their heads like cinder blocks jutted forward. But then, a few miles down the road, rows of cars had pulled over to the side. We asked one woman what they saw in the distance and, first mentioning that she had never seen anything like this, she said that a grizzly bear had caught one of the baby buffalo. In the distance, we could see movement from a dark ghostly figure that must have been the grizzly. After a desultory glance into the distance to clear my conscience, I got back onto the road and drove past all the wandering souls trying to see nature at its most raw. Sadly, a couple miles down the road, we saw more buffalo. Those buffalo were running away from the road heading somewhere off into the distance where the plains met the trees lining the boundary of the forest. Two buffalo butted heads and jammed against each other; one compelling the other not to look back.

Up in Cooke City, winter had never departed. Snow perched atop the pine needles on the pine trees. The road was a slushy mix of snow, mud, and water. Grey and white clouds churned overhead like it was December. And several feet of snowpack lined the sides of the road.

The Beartooth Pass remained closed for the season, but luckily the Chief Joseph Nez Perce Scenic Highway had opened the day before. After clashing with the Army in the Big Hole Valley, Chief Joseph led the Nex Perce down into what is now Yellowstone National Park before they began their improbable trek back north through Montana towards Canada. That morning, we followed the curvy route of the highway down the backside of the Beartooth Mountain Range. Winter turned to spring as we headed down elevation levels and noted how the snowpack receded in our periphery.

After returning to Billings, we were greeted with on-and-off rainstorms for the proceeding days and weeks. A particularly long stretch of torrential rainstorms occurred in early June. After those storms, the temperature quickly rose and we had abnormally hot days for that time of year. Up in the mountains, the hot temperatures melted the way-above-average snowpacks caused by the excessive precipitation. The extreme amount of water in the mountains could not be contained.

The streams in the Beartooth Mountains, already swollen from rain, gushed down into the Yellowstone River. The Lamar and Paradise Valleys, where we had recently traveled through for my daughter's birthday, were now floodplains. Visitors had to be airlifted out of the park by helicopters. Towns on the border of Yellowstone Park, like Gardiner and Red Lodge, were submerged in water. The Yellowstone River pulverized the road that we had traveled weeks before from Gardiner to Mammoth Hot Springs. A battalion of waves wiped away the ground supporting the road, and in some sections the road collapsed into the river. The mad, muddy river swept north to Gardiner. Like a monster, it surged over its banks and wiped out land on either side that had formerly kept it contained. A house teetered on the edge before its front yard finally eroded and the river fully swallowed the house.

Several weeks before the Yellowstone flooded, my dad and I talked about fishing one of the rivers near Billings in late June. A couple weeks after the flooding, the Bighorn was the only river to fish near Billings. My dad and I made a last-minute reservation with an outfitter in Fort Smith and arrived at the river early on a Saturday morning.

Our guide was a young Minnesotan who had guided on the river for the past seven years. He could tell from the instant we met that we wanted to catch a big fish that day. And the conditions were lining up well. The temperature was in the fifties in the morning. The skies had some cloud cover. The river was running at 7,000 cubic feet per second, which was a little high for the river. But, at the same time, it meant that big fish could be hiding in deep holes.

At the access site, a crowd of drift boats floated in the water like boats in a marina. Men and women congregated near the water's edge waiting for their guides to return from parking their trucks. They wore earth-toned fishing pants and colorful fishing shirts. As they waited, trucks backed more boats into the water. A man with a grey handlebar mustache gently slid a classic tan wooden boat into the water and passed by us. One by one, the anglers and guides boarded their boats and drifted away. Next it was our turn.

With the crowd of boats at the access site, it was supposed to take some time for us to spread out and find enough space to fish. There is a rhythm to maneuvering down the river in a boat with a guide.

The guide must slip past other boats while keeping us in good water to fish. As the day stretches on, we eventually should be able to put enough distance between the boats so that we are not right on top of each other. It is bad form to float through a good hole someone else is fishing and spook the fish.

Even though it was supposed to be slow in the morning, we managed to catch several good fish early on. That was mostly due to the conditions on the river. We found plenty of spots either along the banks or the middle of the river where slow and fast water coalesced creating a nice line of water to fish. Throughout the morning, we could count on all our fingers the good-sized brown and rainbow trout that we caught. But we were in search of bigger trout.

Our guide was adept at noticing the little details that the river and fish provided and he knew how to adjust. After catching one brown trout, he quickly pulled out what looked like a tiny turkey baster and sucked out the flies the fish was feasting on. He adjusted the nymphs on our line to match the bugs found in the trout's stomach. He also shifted the weight of the tungsten puddy at the top of the line and the distance between the two flies to match the depth of the water. After catching one smaller-sized rainbow trout, the guide squeezed its mouth and the fish spit out squiggly brown worms that poured all over the guide's pants. Thereafter, the guide switched us to two worms per line instead of flies.

After a few hours, we pulled off into a little channel and stopped for lunch. It was a beautiful morning and we ate our sandwiches as other boats drifted by. While eating, we talked about some of the best books on fly fishing and who nailed the experience in their writing. We compared notes on the works of Maclean to Thomas McGuane to John Gierach. The top prize goes to the author who comes closest to best capturing the experience of fly fishing. Maclean captures the top prize for me, but McGuane's *The Longest Silence* is also a classic.

After lunch, we had miles left of river to fish and it can sometimes be the best time of day to fish. But it can also be hard to catch that first fish after lunch. The food and exposure to the elements have a way of softening your focus. I needed a few jolts of caffeine and gulped down a can of Coke to keep me going.

As we floated, I recalibrated my senses and started paying more attention to the details of the river. The water that flowed over the shallow sections with gravel beneath it had a golden yellow tint. The faster and deeper water in the middle was a darker blue color. The water changed to strips of pure green where the fast water met the slower water near the banks. Farther down, we floated by a section of the river that I had seen displayed in an old-time poster in the fly shop. The outer shells of rusted, old cars lined the right side bank of the river like a cemetery for old cars.

A few minutes later, the yellow bobber on dad's line disappeared down into the deep blue water. The line shook as the fish surged and thrusted underneath. It felt like minutes passed before we could even see the size of the fish on the line. Our guide rowed the boat toward more shallow water along the bank so that he could jump out with a fishing net. As my dad and the fish continued to fight, a fantasia of yellow fins and shiny skin emerged from the darkness. Our guide swooped into action and netted the big brown trout that spun and torqued in the net. The guide picked up the brown trout and I saw the fish's dark black spots spread out like deserted islands on a map. Our guide proudly announced that big brown trout measured 22 inches in length. My dad had caught the big fish of the day. After all the commotion, the big brown trout settled back into the water and rested on the river floor for a minute to regain its strength before swimming into the dark blue water.

What it means to catch the big fish cannot be fully expressed. It is the idea that a fish bigger than all of the rest exists. And you want to be the one that finds it. In fly fishing, there can be no greater feeling than experiencing that moment.

After dad caught the 22 inch brown trout, I turned my attention back to the river and wondered whether I would catch a big fish. Catching two big fish in one day seemed improbable. I had also never seen myself as a lucky person. If experience was any guide, I should just have been happy that one person in our boat caught a big fish. Time was also running out. In a few miles, we would arrive at the take-out spot.

In a flash, my luck changed. My yellow bobber sunk below the surface of the water. The guide screamed to set the hook, but I had already set it. The weight at the end of the line seemed too heavy and the rod tip bent in an almost 90-degree angle. The fish darted back-and-forth in the middle of the river and the guide warned me not to let it break the line off on a stick or rock in the deep water. We needed to get closer to shallow water if we were going to have a chance to bring in the fish.

As the struggle continued, I saw a monster of a fish jump out of the water and splash like a humpback whale. It wriggled in the air and dove back under water. The guide shouted that I needed to make sure the line stayed downstream and I pulled the rod as far upstream as I could. He next rowed us toward shallow water as I reeled the fish in closer. The guide dipped the net into the river and scooped the fish out of the water. The fish's silver dorsal fin extended out of the net as the guide raised it into the air. In the net, I saw a long rainbow trout with a regal stripe of red across its belly. As I wiped the sweat from my forehead, the guide announced the verdict: the rainbow trout measured 21 inches. It was a big fish. I smiled, and then I let the big rainbow trout go.

On the drive back to Billings, I needed more caffeine to keep my eyes open and drank another Coke. It was never easy to drive very far after a long day on the river. I was too tired to say much, other than how lucky we were to both catch a big fish. But the excitement also brought back the memory of another big fish. Dad told the story of when my grandfather caught a giant brown trout on the Big Hole River in June of 1989.

It was the summer that I was first supposed to fish the Big Hole River. The last day of the trip was a cold and snowy day on the river. When my dad and grandfather woke up, they saw six inches of snow on the ground. Half of the group figured they would not be fishing that day, but my grandfather would hear none of it. He told the group that it was "Big Fish Day." Huddled in the warmth of the hotel lobby, my grandfather explained to the group that when the cloud cover is thick and carpets the river, the big fish become more emboldened and active. He went to a local sports store and bought cloth gloves for everyone. He then cut the tips off all the fingers so that everyone could work their fly reels. After getting their supplies and plan in place, my grandfather led the procession of skeptical fly fisherman to Phil Smith's fly shop in Melrose.

At the fly shop, everyone first inspected the rows of colorful flies and tried to pick out something that might work on that gloomy day. The salmonfly hatch continued to be active and almost everyone, including my dad, loaded up on salmonflies and nymphs. But my grandfather was the exception. Phil Smith had told him to buy some large yellow streamers and my grandfather listened. It was as if the river had left an imprint on Phil and my grandfather, and only they could decipher the code. My grandfather tried to convince my dad to buy some yellow streamers too, but they were more expensive than the salmonflies, and besides, the biggest fish ate salmonflies.

The group loaded up into the guides' trucks and drove to the fishing access site at Divide. Six boats went into the river. My dad and my grandfather were the first boat out. Within ten minutes, my dad landed three big trout on the salmonfly nymphs and it looked like he had made the right decision. My grandfather lagged without even a nibble. My dad called to my grandfather in the back of the boat and tried to convince him to switch over to the salmonflies, but my grandfather objected. With the tops of his fingers poking through the winter gloves, he kept casting into the river. He watched his line and stripped back and his spirit rose as he cast out again with all his being.

Five minutes later, something new and magnificent forced itself into existence. When the wondrous brown spots on the of the fish's belly danced above the surface, the spirits of water, fish and flesh moved in unison like flames in a fire. The tightened line confirmed that my grandfather was right to follow the imprint. In that moment, he saw that he had on the line the biggest brown trout that he would ever catch on the Big Hole River. A momentous struggle continued as the trout tried to break away. But the guide became so excited that he allowed the boat the drift into a side channel where the big brown trout could have easily wrapped the line around a willow bush and broke off.

To try to prevent the brown trout from getting away, the guide jumped into the frigid, chest-deep water and held onto the boat to stop it from floating any further down the channel. My grandfather raised his fly rod and reeled the line with one last turn. The big brown trout was close enough to the boat that the guide was able to pull out his fishing net and scoop up the fish. It was twenty-seven inches long and weighed about seven-to-eight pounds, which was a tremendous size for the Big Hole River by any standard. While the giant brown trout wriggled for a moment in the net, the guide and my grandfather went back-and-forth as to what my grandfather would do with the big fish. Would he keep it or release it back into the water? Amid the confusion, the giant brown trout leapt out of the guide's hands and splashed unbeholden to any law on the water's surface. It turned once more out of sight and swam into the river depths. When the moment passed, all that was left was the memory of the moment before the giant trout got away.

After the trip, the giant trout became part of local lore. In fly shops and bars, fishermen talked about the giant trout that George McCarthy caught one snowy June day when the yellow streamer outmatched the salmonfly. George, the local boy from Butte, who moved to Washington, D.C. to work for the President. The giant trout that Phil Smith had in his hands before it slipped away. And Phil was a good one, he knew the river better than any guide. That monster with bright spots like fading stars from a faraway galaxy. It may still be swimming in a deep hole in the river, they said. Some people even told the story as if they were fishing with my grandfather in the boat that day. They wanted to feel connected to something wonderful.

It took years for me to learn how to fly fish and I am still not close to the type of fly fisherman my grandfather was. Countless hours spent on a riverbank or in a boat watching a fly drift by without a nibble. Countless hours practicing the form of the cast until it became ingrained in my mind. The rainbow trout I caught on the Bighorn was not as big as the giant brown trout my grandfather caught on the Big Hole. But when my dad told the story about my grandfather, I felt connected to something wonderful, too.

TWENTY-FIVE

RETURNING HOME

In the fall of 2022, I accepted an offer for a new job in New Jersey. It was difficult to leave Montana, but we packed up our belongings into the largest truck that U-Haul offered and drove it across the country in under a week. I was mindful that this was the second time someone from my family had packed a family into a car to move all the way across the country. In 1961, my grandfather had done the same. But he never left Montana, and I do not think it is possible that Montana could ever leave me.

Back in New Jersey, our family moved into a neighborhood with nice homes and good schools. But life in New Jersey was more crowded and congested than Montana. There were not the same wide-open spaces to roam and explore. At times, I missed the majestic rivers of Montana.

The next summer, I planned another fly fishing trip to Montana with my friends from college. We only had two days to fish the

Big Hole, but that was enough. The first day we fished the canyon section of the river and did well. During the morning of the first day, I caught a nice-sized brown trout with a golden belly that was worth a picture.

The next day, we floated the more wide-open section of the river below Melrose. The fishing was good in the morning, but it slowed in the afternoon. The fish were lethargic and we drifted down the river without even a nibble on a fly. Then our guide wisely pulled the drift boat near a bubbly creek that connected with the river. A foam line formed where the creek and river met. The guide directed me to cast up the creek and let the fly drift down. Without a bite, I kept casting the fly above the foam line. At first, my mind hurried with the hope of catching a fish. I casted over and over without a response each time. But then I let all worry fade away and enjoyed the experience. When I let go is when something happened. As the line suddenly tightened, a colorful rainbow trout swallowed the fly and whirled in the water next to the boat. The guide swooped up the shiny trout and a new memory on the river was formed.

When we let go of worry, we open ourselves up to wonder. We live in a world enveloped by technology. We are connected to computers, tablets, and phones during almost every moment of our wakeful existence. Our devices connect us to more data than we can truly comprehend. Being constantly distracted by technology affects how we live and see the world. In a world full of distraction, it can be difficult to find a place to escape and let go.

My plan at the beginning of the pandemic was to focus more on fly fishing so that I could find some tranquility and freedom, and I accomplished that goal. Fishing the Big Hole River and other rivers in Montana provided plenty of tranquility and freedom. But it also provided more than that. Fly fishing and spending time on the river provided consolation in a difficult time. Spending time on the river was a healing experience, and it offered a chance to grow and adapt. I was grateful to live in a place that afforded me the opportunity to explore and connect with the outside world.

During my fly fishing journey, I also learned that it takes practice to learn how to be present on the river. When I first learned to fly fish, I would constantly focus on how to cast and where to aim the fly. But to be present on the river, I first had to become proficient enough at fly fishing for the act itself to fade into the back of my mind. Once I became good enough at fly fishing, the act of casting or reading the water became an innate experience. I could do it without focusing on it. And once I learned how to become good enough at fly fishing, time slowed down and I had the chance to reflect and be present. I could be more open to the sublime feeling of being immersed in nature and take in the majestic environment around me.

After decades of fly fishing, I am far from perfect at it. But, for me, fly fishing is not about being perfect. The key is to let go of what is not important and remember what is. Fly fishing allows me to forget distractions and instead remember what matters in life. It brings back memories of the thrill of my first trout on the line and time spent with my dad, grandfather, and uncle Joe. It reminds me of the guide who first taught me to fish, Phil Smith, and the photo of him that I was able pass on to his daughter. Those memories remain with the river.

The river is like poetry, my grandfather once said. It leaves an imprint on your soul. Listen and you will understand. Some things are worth holding on to.

AFTERWORD

A lot has changed since I wrote down the stories in this book. Our family has grown. We bought a new home. We now live thousands of miles away from the rivers that I wrote about in these stories. But, looking back, I am glad that I took the time to write down my experiences. Reading these stories reminds me of how peaceful it can be to spend a few hours fishing on a river in Montana.

These stories only capture a small snapshot of time. One slow morning or afternoon on a river does not mean that it is the way it will always be. It is not every day that an angler catches a giant trout. There are too many factors to consider. Overall, though, my good days have far outnumbered my tough days fly fishing. The best advice is probably to fish a river as many days as you can. Eventually your luck will start to even out.

My first trip to the Big Hole River served as inspiration for this book. Parts of this book describe challenges that the river faces. Four years after writing these stories, though, it seems like there are some encouraging signs. A quick Google search reveals that more recent surveys have shown the trout population has increased. The state has also invested millions of dollars into preserving the river. Those are good steps.

It is stereotypical to think of the American West as a place of rugged individualism. But success is due to the cooperation of many people, not one person. Hopefully local community members and state leaders will continue to cooperate to preserve the natural habitat of rivers in Montana.

It is impossible to capture fly fishing in Montana through words alone. But writing this book has been a rewarding journey of its own. I wrote so much about rivers that they became like old friends. Far away now, but not forgotten. Ready to pick up where we left off the next time we meet.

ENDNOTES

1. Maclean, Norman. *A River Runs Through It and Other Stories*. The University of Chicago Press, 2017, p. 119.
2. Howard, Joseph Kinsey. *Montana high, wide and handsome*. University of Nebraska Press, 2003, pp. 85-101.
3. Maclean, p. 4.
4. Nerburn, Kent. *Chief Joseph & The Flight of the Nez Perce*. HarperOne, 2005. (Used for all background on the Battle of the Big Hole).
5. Egan, Timothy. *The Immortal Irishman: The Irish Revolutionary Who Became an American Hero*. Houghton Mifflin Harcourt, 2016. (Used for all background on Thomas Francis Meagher).
6. Mansch, Scott. "Benny Reynolds: A Montana rodeo legend remembered." *Great Falls Tribune*, February 23, 2014.
7. www.prorodeohalloffame.com/inductees/all-around/benny-reynolds/
8. Gibbons, Mark. "The Kid." *Mostly Cloudy*. FootHills Publishing, 2020, p. 18.
9. Stegner, Wallace. "Genesis." *Wolf Willow*. Penguin Books, 2000.
10. Sexton, John. *Baseball as a Road to God - Seeing Beyond the Game*. Gotham Books, 2013, pp. 28-30.
11. Whitman, Walt. "Song of Myself (1892 Version)." *Poetry Foundation*, www.poetryfoundation.org/poems/45477/song-of-myself-1892-version
12. Adams, Duncan. "Wise River endures a long summer of heat, smoke and uncertainty." *Montana Standard*, August 9, 2021.
13. Robbins, Jim. "Montana's Famed Trout Under Threat as Drought Intensifies." *New York Times*, July 23, 2021.

14. Warren, Chris. *Ernest Hemingway in the Yellowstone High Country.* Riverbend Publishing, 2019, p. 9.
15. Warren, p. 84.
16. Warren, p. 18.
17. Warren, p. 51.
18. Warren, p. 9.
19. Warren, p. 18-19.
20. Warren, p. 69.
21. Warren, p. 19.
22. Warren, p. 13.
23. Warren, p. 104.
24. Lyons, Nick. *Hemingway on Fishing.* Scribner, 2000, pp. 135-137.

Other Sources

I also used the following sources for the subjects listed below.

<u>William and Huguette Clark</u>:

Dedman, Bill and Newell, Jr., Paul Clark. *Empty Mansions: The Mysterious Life of Huguette Clark and the Spending of a Great American Fortune.* Ballantine Books, 2014.

<u>Big Hole River</u>:

Munday, Pat. *Montana's Last Best River: The Big Hole and Its People.* Globe Pequot Press, 2001.

<u>Butte and the Speculator Mine Disaster</u>:

Punke, Michael. *Fire and Brimstone: The North Butte Mining Disaster of 1917.* HarperCollins Publishers, 2016.

<u>Virginia City and Montana Vigilantes</u>:

Allen, Frederick. *A Decent, Orderly Lynching: Montana Vigilantes.* University of Oklahoma Press, 2004.

ACKNOWLEDGMENTS

Thanks to Daniel J. Rice and Riverfeet Press for providing the opportunity to publish this book. Daniel's edits and insights have been invaluable, and this book would not be possible without his efforts.

Thank you to my parents. I would not have had the chance to fly fish and explore Montana without their support. I am grateful for all the memories we have together in Montana.

My grandfather paved the way for this book. He led an extraordinary life and accomplished many things throughout his career. But he always put his family first. And he loved Montana and its people.

Most of my time fly fishing has been spent floating the Big Hole River with a guide. I became better at fly fishing because of the lessons learned from those guides and I am thankful for their help.

Last, but not least, this book would not be possible without the support of my wife, Samantha. She gave me the time to write these stories and has kept our growing family together. One day I hope to pass on the experience of fly fishing to Billie Grace and Declan as well.

Brendan McCarthy is an angler, attorney and author. As a teenager, Brendan learned to fly fish from his dad and grandfather who were both born and raised in Butte, Montana. Brendan then moved to Billings, Montana in 2013, and continued to explore the rivers of Montana. *Arc of the River* captures the experience of fly fishing over the past thirty years in the state known as the Last Best Place.

Brendan graduated from the University of Notre Dame and Notre Dame Law School. He now lives in Princeton Junction, New Jersey with his wife, two children, and dog, Bo.

Other titles from Riverfeet Press

RIVERFEET

printed in the USA
www.riverfeetpress.com